Thriving In Transition: Your Roadmap for Life's Seasons

By Xavian D. Lewis

Thriving In Transition: Your Roadmap for Life's Seasons

Table of Contents

Dedication

To my mother and father, who taught me that transition is not an ending, but an invitation to grow, become, and thrive.

Author's Note

This book was not written from a place of having everything figured out. It was written from the middle — the in-between seasons where life is shifting, identity is being reshaped, and certainty feels just out of reach. Thriving In Transition was born out of real moments of disruption, reflection, prayer, and growth — seasons where I had to learn how to trust God not only in the promise of what was coming, but in the uncertainty of where I stood.

Transitions have a way of exposing us. They reveal what we've built our identity on, what we fear losing, and what we're being invited to release. I wrote this book for anyone who has felt the tension of becoming — those standing at the crossroads of change, wondering if what feels like an ending might actually be the beginning of something greater.

This is not a book to rush through. It is meant to be read slowly, honestly, and reflectively. Some chapters may feel timely; others may feel uncomfortable. I encourage you to pause when needed, revisit sections as seasons change, and allow the lessons to meet you where you are — not where you think you should be.

My hope is that these pages remind you of this truth: you are not behind, broken, or forgotten. You are in process. And every season you walk through carries purpose, even when it doesn't make sense yet.

May this book serve as a companion as you navigate the shifts of life — and may you discover that you are not merely surviving transition, but learning how to thrive within it.

Xavian D. Lewis

Chapter 1: Embracing Change: The Foundation of Thriving

When Life Refuses to Stay the Same

Change will break you if you don't learn how to bend. That's the truth many of us spend years resisting. We cling to routines, relationships, and identities as if they are permanent—as if life owes us predictability. But life does not negotiate with our preferences. It shifts, often without warning, and demands that we shift with it. Change does not enter politely. It storms in like a hurricane, rattling the windows of your inner world, scattering the furniture of your plans, and daring you to stand in the wreckage. Yet hidden inside the chaos is an invitation: the chance to discover who you really are once the familiar has been stripped away. Every season of life begins and ends with change. You cannot control when it arrives, but you can choose how you move through it. You can resist, gripping tightly to what is already slipping away, or you can release your hold and allow transition to carry you toward what is next. I've lived through seasons that stole my breath—moments where I whispered, This cannot be the plan. But time revealed a deeper truth: what broke me also built me. What felt like an ending was often a beginning in disguise. Before we talk about renewal, optimism, growth, healing, or thriving, we must start here—with change. Because when change is misunderstood, every season feels like punishment instead of preparation. Change isn't your enemy. It's the soil where your destiny takes root. And once you begin to see it that way, disruption stops feeling like an attack and starts revealing itself as formation.

Section 1: Understanding the Nature of Change

When the Ground Beneath You Moves

Change is the quiet architect shaping the story of your life. It redraws the blueprint of your existence without asking permission. You can't vote against it, legislate it away, or pretend it isn't happening. Change moves like shifting tectonic plates—slow, subtle, almost invisible—until suddenly the ground quakes and nothing looks the same. At first, change feels like chaos. It disrupts your rhythm, unsettles your plans, and challenges your sense of control. What once felt stable begins to wobble. What you expected to last starts to fade. Disorientation sets in, and it can feel as though life itself has turned against you. But what you call chaos, life often calls construction. Change rarely tears something down without making room for something new to rise. Consider a forest fire. To the untrained eye, it looks like destruction—charred ground, scorched trees, and loss. Yet in nature, fire is often necessary. It releases seeds trapped in cones, enriches the soil, and creates the precise conditions required for new life. What looks like devastation is actually preparation. So it is with you. The flames of change may roar through your life, but buried in the ashes are seeds of a future you couldn't see before. Seasons of instability are often seasons of divine rearrangement—where God is quietly rebuilding the capacity of your life. You may not recognize it while the smoke is thick, but with time, new possibilities begin to emerge where old plans once stood. Change, at its core, is not just about what leaves—it's about what becomes possible.

The Fire That Frees You

We cling desperately to what we know—even when what we know is too small for who we are becoming. Familiarity feels safe, even when it limits us. We hold on to old roles, expired relationships, unhelpful habits, and outdated versions of ourselves simply because they are familiar. But disruption loosens your grip on what can no longer sustain your growth. Pain is not always punishment. Sometimes, it is pruning. The fire of change removes what cannot follow you into the next season. It exposes what you've outgrown and illuminates what no longer fits. It reveals where you've been settling, shrinking, or hiding. The job that no longer fulfills you. The relationship that drains more than it gives. The identity built on other people's expectations. Change places these things under a holy spotlight. And while loss is painful, it clears the space necessary for expansion. If you measure change only by what it takes away, it will always feel like an enemy. But when you measure it by what it makes possible, your relationship with transition begins to shift. The fire does not come to leave you empty. It comes to burn away what is false, unhealthy, or finished, so what is true, aligned, and life-giving can finally take shape. Pruning never feels kind in the moment—but it is the very thing that ensures greater growth later.

Why Change Feels Like Resistance

Disruption feels like resistance because it presses against the parts of you that want to stay the same. It's easier to cling to what you know than to trust what you haven't yet seen. When routines are interrupted and comfort is challenged, your instinct is to protect the familiar. That's human. But comfort is not the same as calling. What feels "normal" can quietly become the very thing keeping you small. When you focus only on what change removes, every shift feels like loss. You assume God is withholding, life is unfair, or you've failed somehow. But when you begin to see change as clarity, everything shifts. Disruption loosens what you've outgrown but refused to release. It exposes the fragility of what you once trusted—your plans, your security, even your identity—and invites you to build on something stronger. Some doors closed not because you were unworthy, but because the rooms behind them were too small for who you are becoming. Change is not cruelty; it is clarity. It reveals what is temporary so you can anchor yourself in what is eternal. It exposes where you placed your identity in things never meant to define you. And while loss may still sting, clarity gives you vision—helping you see that within every disruption is an invitation to grow deeper, trust further, and become more whole.

Real-World Analogy: The River Crossing

Imagine standing at the edge of a wide river. Behind you is everything familiar—routines, patterns, and safe choices you know by heart. Ahead is the land of your becoming—unknown, yet full of promise. The crossing is the part no one prepares you for. The water is cold. The ground is uneven. The current presses against you, and halfway through, you're tempted to turn back, questioning why you ever left the safety of the shore. But the in-between is where transformation happens. Growth isn't found in what you left behind or in what lies ahead—it is forged in the crossing itself. In that tension, your faith stretches, your fear is confronted, and your capacity expands. You learn to loosen your grip on control and place deeper trust in the One guiding your steps. The river does not drown you; it develops you. The resistance strengthens you. The uncertainty trains your trust. And when you finally step onto the other side, you realize the greatest change isn't your location—it's you.

What This Season Is Trying to Teach You

Change is never random. Every shaking, every disruption, every closed door carries purpose. This season is not here to strip you—it's here to prepare you. It may be exposing misplaced identity, misaligned priorities, or areas where your faith must deepen. It may be calling you out of familiar cycles and inviting you into a version of yourself you've hesitated to become. When you begin asking, *"What is this season teaching me?"* instead of *"Why is this happening to me?"* you move from victimhood into growth. Reflection turns chaos into curriculum. You stop merely enduring change and start extracting wisdom from it—discernment, resilience, clarity, and self-awareness rising where confusion once lived. Now that you understand why change comes and how it moves, the question becomes this: *how do you posture your mind to thrive within it?* How do you think, believe, and perceive in ways that support your becoming instead of sabotaging it? That is where we go next.

Section 2: Embracing a Growth Mindset

When God Asks You to Release

Loss is never just loss—it is a divine invitation. Every season of growth will ask something from you. Sometimes it asks gently. Sometimes it asks abruptly. But it always asks. The familiar must be surrendered for the future to unfold. And here's the spiritual tension: we cry out for transformation but refuse to release what prevents it. We want new without letting go of old. We want doors to open while we cling to doorways that have already closed. You cannot hold on to the past and step fully into purpose at the same time. A clenched fist cannot grow. A growth mindset isn't just positive thinking; it is spiritual positioning. It is the posture that allows you to see loss as redirection and discomfort as preparation. It's not about pretending everything feels good. It's about trusting that everything can be used for good. My pastor, Mark Ellis Sr., D. Div., once said, *"God will never require something He isn't willing to return better."* That truth has carried me through many transitions. When God asks you to release something—a relationship, a role, a dream, a plan—it is not deprivation. It is divine exchange. What leaves your hands may feel like loss, but what returns is refined, elevated, and aligned with your next season. Release is not God taking from you. Release is God making room for you.

The Exchange God Requires

A growth mindset is rooted in the belief that God is intentional with every exchange. It shifts your thinking from "God is taking something away" to "God is trading this for something better suited to my future." When you're in the middle of transition, that can be hard to see. The job you lost, the relationship that ended, the opportunity that slipped away—they all feel final. But in the Kingdom, endings are rarely just endings; they are often repositionings. When you choose a growth mindset, you allow God to reinterpret your losses. You begin to ask, "What is this making possible? What is this freeing me from? What is this freeing me for?" The exchange may not make sense at first. You'll have days where grief screams louder than faith. That's okay. A growth mindset doesn't demand that you skip grief—it simply refuses to let grief become your permanent address. It holds space for both sorrow and expectation, both questions and trust.

When Perspective Becomes Your Power

Perspective does not change what happened, but it changes how what happened shapes you. A growth mindset teaches you to shift the story you tell yourself. Instead of saying, "I failed," you begin to ask, "What did this experience teach me?" Instead of, "Why did this happen to me?" you shift to, "Who am I becoming because of this?" You move from self-blame to self-awareness, from shame to stewardship. This kind of thinking doesn't mean you minimize the pain or pretend you're unaffected. It simply means you refuse to waste it. You allow hard moments to deepen your compassion, sharpen your boundaries, and refine your discernment. Your perspective becomes your power because it determines whether experiences crush you or cultivate you. You may not control the storm, but you control the meaning you give it.

Real-World Analogy: Social Media & Shifting Circles

Think about social media. Someone unfollows you, or you unfollow someone. At first, it feels personal—like rejection or distance. But often, it's alignment. People shift because seasons shift. Circles evolve because your calling evolves. Some people are assigned to your life for a chapter, not the whole book. When you insist on dragging them into every season, you create weight God never intended you to carry. Your career works the same way. Being overlooked for a promotion or rejected from a job isn't always failure; sometimes it's rerouting. The doors that don't open reveal the doors you were never meant to walk through. What feels like loss may be strategic repositioning. With a growth mindset, you stop obsessing over who left and what didn't work, and you start paying attention to how God is making room for what actually fits you.

The Shift Beneath Your Surface

A growth mindset does not remove the pain of change—it reframes it. It teaches you to see beyond your immediate discomfort and recognize the beginnings hidden underneath. There is a quiet shift happening beneath the surface of your life right now. You may not see it, but you can feel it—the sense that you are outgrowing certain patterns, that your perspective is widening, that your tolerance for misalignment is shrinking. That's not you "being difficult." That's you evolving. Endings start to feel less like punishments and more like confirmations that you are ready for more. You realize you no longer fit inside the spaces that once contained you. And that awareness is a sign that transformation is already underway. Now that your perspective is shifting, there is one more layer to explore: how endings ignite transformation. That leads us into one of the greatest truths about transition.

Section 3: Recognizing the Potential for Positive Transformation

When Life Breaks Without Warning

Sometimes life takes something you love without warning. A relationship ends. A plan collapses. A dream dissolves. It feels like betrayal—like the ground has opened beneath you. You find yourself replaying conversations, questioning decisions, doubting your worth, and wondering where God is in all of it. What feels like devastation is often the soil of your deepest becoming. Some endings feel violent—sudden, sharp, and unfair. They don't come with closure or explanation. They just… end. In those moments, it's natural to feel like everything is over. But if you stay in that place long enough to breathe, to reflect, and to listen, you discover a painful gift: the break exposes what you were never meant to build your identity on. I remember a relationship I believed would last forever. I invested everything—love, time, energy, dreams. I built a future in my head around a person who, in my mind, was already my spouse. And then one day, without warning, it was over. The ending felt like a blade—swift, merciless, disorienting. It wasn't just heartbreak; it was identity collapse. I questioned everything: myself, God, and the plans I thought were secure. But time revealed something I couldn't see in the moment: I had tied my worth to someone else's presence. The ending forced me to face the parts of myself I had ignored. The blade didn't sever my future; it freed it.

The Soil of Self-Discovery

Endings create space for beginnings. What feels like ruin often becomes revelation. Pain demands that you look inward. Loss invites you to examine what you've been standing on. Disappointment forces you to discover who you are without the roles, people, or plans you once depended on. Transformation rarely feels gentle. It feels like chiseling. It feels like pruning. It feels like breaking. But the sculptor never wounds without purpose. Life chips away only what cannot follow you into your destiny. In the aftermath of an ending, you begin to ask new questions: Who am I now? What do I truly value? What was I ignoring while I was trying so hard to hold everything together? Slowly, you realize that what broke you also built you. You discover strengths that would have stayed hidden if everything had gone according to your original script. You find new parts of yourself in the rubble of what you lost.

Real-World Analogy: Leveling Up

Life can be compared to a video game. Each job, relationship, or season is a level. Sometimes you get knocked out of a level abruptly—losing points, progress, or momentum. It feels unfair, especially when you thought you were close to "winning." But failure forces you to learn. Loss forces you to grow. Rejection forces you to develop strategy. You do not progress because you are perfect. You progress because you persist. The next level demands a version of you the last level could not produce. The skills you need later are often forged in the challenges you face now. With each "game over," you return wiser, sharper, and more equipped. In the same way, life's hardest hits can become the training ground for your greatest victories. What knocked you down in one season can become the very thing that propels you higher in the next.

Rising From the Ruins

Pain does not come to punish; it comes to prepare. It arrives like an uninvited messenger, carrying lessons you would never have sought but desperately needed. Pain is a sculptor — chiseling away what no longer belongs, shaping the edges of your character, maturing your discernment, and revealing the parts of you that were dormant or underdeveloped. It stretches your understanding, expands your emotional capacity, and strengthens the muscles of faith you didn't even know you had. Endings, as painful as they are, refine your judgment. They sharpen the clarity of your "yes" and strengthen the conviction of your "no." They teach you how to see beyond the surface — how to recognize authenticity, how to identify subtle red flags, how to detect alignment and misalignment quicker than before. Endings force you to pay attention to what your spirit has been whispering but your emotions have been ignoring. They expose the patterns you've outgrown and the cycles you can no longer afford to repeat. Endings deepen your capacity to love — not by making you harder, but by making you wiser. They teach you how to love without losing yourself, how to care without collapsing, how to give without emptying to the point of depletion. They strengthen the boundaries that protect your peace, your purpose, and your identity. Pain teaches you the difference between relationships that nourish you and relationships that drain you; between environments that grow you and environments that shrink you. It adjusts your vision so you can recognize sincerity and reject performance, choose purpose over attachment, and value alignment over availability. And now that you understand how transformation emerges from endings, you are ready to step into the next season with clarity and courage. Because endings, no matter how devastating, are not the conclusion — they are the clearing. They create the space your future needs. They remove what cannot grow with you. They free the ground for something new to take root.

A Gentle Turn Toward Spring

As the day settles and you reflect on what you've learned, remember this: change is not your adversary; it is your evolution. The seasons of life will continue to shift—some softly, some violently—but every shift carries meaning. You are rooted deeper than you think. What you have survived has strengthened your foundation. What you have lost has created space for what will be gained. Picture a tree in winter. Bare branches. Cold ground. Silent air. Yet beneath the soil, life is stirring. Roots are expanding. Seeds are swelling. The earth is quietly preparing for the thaw. That is where you are now. You've learned how to embrace change. You've begun to see disruption as construction, endings as openings, and pain as preparation. Now it's time to learn how to think differently inside it. Spring is not just a season; it is a mindset. It is the courage to believe in better even when life still looks barren. It is the discipline of planting seeds when the ground does not yet show promise. Turn the page. Spring is calling.

Chapter 2: Spring Renewal: Cultivating a Positive Mindset

When Hope Begins Beneath the Surface

Here's the truth: negativity is cheap, but optimism is costly. Anyone can slip into cynicism, rehearsing every disappointment until the mind becomes a graveyard of what-ifs and could-have-beens. Anyone can expect the worst because expecting nothing requires no courage. But optimism? That is expensive. It demands bravery. It requires spiritual stamina. It is choosing to plant seeds of possibility in soil that still looks barren, trusting that what is unseen is still unfolding. Optimism is not naïve positivity — it is disciplined faith. It is the strength to believe in better even when every circumstance screams "give up." And when life shifts beneath your feet, when you're in a season of transition and nothing feels stable, optimism becomes the difference between quitting too soon and staying long enough to witness the first signs of change emerging from the dirt. Without optimism, you walk blindly into despair, convinced that what you see now is all there will ever be. With optimism, you begin to sense the future forming before it manifests. You catch glimpses of what could be — not because you see it yet, but because you believe it's possible. Spring is the season when the earth warms just enough for seeds to swell beneath the surface. Before any bloom breaks through, there is a sacred, hidden transformation happening in darkness. That is what optimism is: the inner work that takes place before anything in your life looks different. It is the faith that begins beneath the surface, preparing you for what will eventually rise. Let's dig into the soil of your inner world and learn how to plant what your future needs.

Section 1: Planting Seeds of Optimism

When Your Mind Decides What Grows

Without optimism, you will bury yourself in fear long before life ever buries you in failure. Fear is a terrible gardener — it plants doubt, nurtures insecurity, and convinces you that nothing good can grow in your life. Fear whispers that trying is pointless, that dreaming is dangerous, that wanting more is unrealistic. But optimism plants something entirely different: vision, expectation, and possibility. It conditions the soil of your spirit so that transformation has somewhere to take root. Just like spring, optimism never begins with brightness; it begins with belief. Before the sunlight hits the ground, before the rain nourishes the seed, before the petals unfold, something must shift in the soil. Something must choose to grow.

The Weight of What You Choose to Plant

Optimism does not happen by accident — it happens by choice. A farmer never wanders into a field hoping crops magically appear. They plant intentionally, understanding that what is sown will eventually determine the harvest. You do the same with your thoughts. You choose what gets planted, and you choose what gets nurtured. Seeds of pessimism produce weeds — weeds that choke out confidence, creativity, perseverance, and joy. Seeds of optimism produce fruit — resilience, hope, endurance, faith, and vision for the future. And when you're between the ages of 18 and 25, the soil of life is wildly unpredictable. Student loans, identity questions, friendships shifting, relationships being tested, first jobs that feel shaky, schedules that constantly change, and the pressure to "get it right." Nothing feels steady. Planting anything — hope, dreams, or intention — feels risky. But hear this clearly: *Seeds grow best in uncertain soil.* It is the instability that pushes them deeper. It is the unfamiliar ground that demands stronger roots. It is the discomfort that makes them stretch until they break through the surface. Your life is no different. God uses the instability of your early seasons to anchor you in ways comfort never could.

Seeing Beyond the Storm

Optimism is not escapism — it is the holy reframing of reality. It doesn't ignore the storm; it sees through it. Picture yourself driving on a highway during heavy rain. Visibility is low, the road feels dangerous, and you can't see more than a few feet ahead. But optimism is your high beam — it doesn't illuminate the entire route, but it gives you just enough clarity to keep moving forward. Without optimism, you pull over and stop.
With optimism, you keep driving because you trust that storms are temporary. Optimism whispers a timeless truth your fear will never tell you: *"This moment is not the whole story."*

The First Seed Is Always Belief

All transformation begins with one simple but profound decision: belief.

Belief that something good can grow out of your current season. Belief that where you are is not where you will stay. Belief that your story is unfinished, unfolding, and continually being shaped by God's timing. Without belief, nothing grows. Without planting, nothing changes. Optimism is the seed — planted before any bloom appears, planted before anything looks hopeful, planted before there is any evidence you're moving forward. And here's the miracle of belief: it multiplies. One seed becomes two. Two become ten. Before long, the inner landscape of your life transforms into a garden you never thought possible.

What Spring Is Teaching You Already

Planting optimism is not wishful thinking — it is spiritual courage. It is choosing life, choosing hope, choosing God's promises even when life feels against you. It is the bold declaration that your story still has room to bloom. But planting is only the beginning. Because once seeds are planted, they must be nurtured. And that is where we go next.

Section 2: Nurturing a Mindset for Growth

When Small Thinking Shrinks Your Future

If your mind stays small, your future will too. Nothing in your life will expand beyond the boundaries of your thinking. A constricted mind produces a constricted life, limiting not only what you pursue but what you believe is even possible for you. When your perspective is rooted in fear, doubt, or past limitation, it quietly suffocates opportunity before you ever take a step toward it. You begin to disqualify yourself from rooms you've never entered, conversations you've never had, and possibilities God has already placed within your reach. The truth is, nothing changes until the way you think changes. Your life will only rise to the level of your belief. If you see yourself as stuck, you will move like someone who is stuck. If you see yourself as incapable, you will avoid the very opportunities that require your growth. But when your thinking begins to expand, your vision expands with it. You start to recognize that what once felt impossible may have simply been unfamiliar. Growth does not begin with action—it begins with belief. It is the quiet, internal decision that more is available, that more is achievable, and that more is within reach when you partner with God. Before you ever move your feet, your mind must agree with your future. Because the life you are called to live will always require a mindset big enough to sustain it.

The Two Voices That Shape Your Becoming

Every young adult carries two internal voices, often competing for control in the quiet moments of decision. One is the fixed mindset, whispering, *"This is who I am, and I cannot change,"* convincing you that your past defines your future and that your limitations are permanent. The other is the growth mindset, declaring, *"This is who I am, but I am capable of becoming more,"* reminding you that who you are today is not the final version of who you're called to be. The difference between these voices may feel subtle in the moment, but the consequences are profound over time. A fixed mindset chains you to insecurity, paralyzes you in fear, and transforms every failure into identity, making you believe that mistakes are reflections of your worth rather than moments of development. But a growth mindset interprets failure differently—it sees it as information, as feedback, as a classroom shaping your next move rather than a verdict sealing your fate. For young adults stepping into the unknown—navigating purpose, relationships, finances, and identity—this shift changes everything. Growth reframes roadblocks as redirection, confusion as curiosity, and fear as fuel that propels you forward instead of holding you back. Over time, your mindset becomes your map, quietly guiding your decisions, shaping your confidence, and determining the risks you are willing to take. And the map you carry ultimately determines the places you allow yourself to go, the opportunities you embrace, and the version of yourself you give permission to become.

A Garden That Responds to Its Gardener

Carol Dweck said it beautifully: *"Becoming is better than being."* And that truth carries more weight than most people realize, because becoming requires something that being does not—it requires movement, vulnerability, and flexibility. It demands that you release the illusion of arrival and embrace the reality of process. Becoming asks you to lean into the unknown, to stretch beyond your comfort, and to trust that progress is not a threat to your identity but a gift to your future. When you commit to becoming, you give yourself permission to evolve, to grow beyond old limitations, and to step into versions of yourself that once felt out of reach. Think of your mind as soil—alive, responsive, and constantly producing something based on what you plant within it. If you consistently plant negativity, fear, and doubt, weeds will grow, choking out your confidence, your creativity, and your courage before they ever have a chance to flourish. But when you intentionally plant courage, curiosity, discipline, and vision, something beautiful begins to push through the surface, even if it takes time to be seen. What you nurture will always thrive, and what you neglect or starve will inevitably wither. Your thoughts are not passive—they are powerful, and they function as seeds shaping the landscape of your life. Whether you realize it or not, you are always planting something, and over time, your inner world will reflect exactly what you have chosen to cultivate.

Rewriting the Story Your Mind Has Told You

A growth mindset does more than open you to possibility—it rewrites the narrative you've been telling yourself about your life. What once felt like rejection begins to reveal itself as redirection, guiding you away from spaces that could not sustain your growth. What once felt like loss starts to function as a launch, pushing you into new territory you may have never chosen on your own. What once felt like failure becomes a foundation, providing the lessons, strength, and perspective needed to build something stronger and more aligned. In this shift, what once felt like subtraction begins to look like shaping. You start to realize that life is not taking from you—it is transforming you. When you adopt a growth mindset, you stop interpreting endings as evidence of inadequacy, and instead begin to see them as divine rerouting toward environments, opportunities, and relationships that better match your calling. You no longer panic at change—you partner with it. You no longer fear disruption—you learn from it. Staying open becomes your superpower, because openness creates the space for God to move, to refine, and to reveal what you could not see before. And in that openness, you discover that every ending was not a loss—it was alignment in disguise.

The Quiet Work Beneath Your Becoming

Growth doesn't happen on accident — it is intentional. It is the outcome of every choice you make, every perspective you challenge, every belief you unlearn, and every truth you dare to embrace. Growth is not a passive evolution; it is an active pursuit. It stretches you, confronts you, and reintroduces you to parts of yourself you didn't know were there. And once your mindset begins to shift and expand, once your thinking evolves and your perspective widens, something sacred becomes possible: resilience. Because every seed you plant — every hopeful thought, every disciplined habit, every courageous decision — and every mindset you nurture will inevitably meet resistance. Not because you're doing something wrong, but because you're doing something right. Growth always attracts pressure. Becoming always invites friction. Every new level demands a stronger foundation, and resistance is how that foundation is built. Resistance is not a sign to retreat; it is a signal that transformation is underway. It is the gym where your faith is strengthened, the classroom where your endurance is taught, the battlefield where your insecurities are confronted, and the soil where your character is rooted. And it is inside that resistance — inside the discomfort, the stretching, the uncertainty — that the real becoming begins.

Section 3: Fostering Resilience in the Face of Change

When Life's Pressure Forces You to Strengthen

If you don't learn to bend, life will break you.
Because life is not gentle with structures that refuse to move. It will push, stretch, and pull you in directions you never anticipated. And if your spirit is rigid, if your mind is inflexible, if your heart refuses to adjust, the pressure of transition will crack the very parts of you that God designed to grow. Resilience is not about being unbreakable; it is about learning the sacred art of bending without losing your roots. It is the quiet strength of remaining grounded when everything around you is shifting. It is the ability to withstand the winds of change without surrendering your identity, your integrity, your purpose, or your faith. Resilience is not the absence of pain — it is the refusal to allow that pain to define you. Every soul that grows will face storms. Not mild breezes, but winds strong enough to test the depth of your roots. Every life that expands will encounter pressure — the kind that squeezes truth out of you and forces you to confront who you really are beneath the surface. And it is in those moments, those spiritually seismic moments, that resilience becomes the bridge between who you were and who you are becoming. Because on one side stands the version of you that survived. But on the other side is the version of you that will thrive. And resilience is how you get from here to there — bending, adapting, trusting, enduring, and rising stronger than the storm that tried to break you.

What Resistance Is Really Teaching You

Life will stretch you in ways you never asked for, pulling you beyond the boundaries of comfort and into spaces that feel unfamiliar, uncertain, and sometimes overwhelming. It will push you out of what feels safe, shake loose what no longer fits, and confront you with realities you cannot ignore. But what feels like resistance is not punishment—it is preparation. It is life strengthening you for what your next season will require. Think of a tree in a hurricane. The winds are violent, relentless, and unforgiving. The weaker branches snap under pressure, unable to withstand the force. But the trunk—the deeply rooted, grounded part—does not resist the wind in rigidity; it bends, it yields, and yet it rises again. That is resilience. It is not the absence of pain or pressure—it is the ability to endure it without losing your foundation. It is bending without breaking, hurting without quitting, and falling without disappearing. It is the quiet strength that allows you to remain anchored in who you are, even when everything around you is shifting.

The Beauty in Being Put Back Together

Kintsugi—the Japanese art of restoring broken pottery with gold—reveals a profound truth about your life: *what was once broken does not have to be hidden; it can be made beautiful.* Instead of disguising the cracks, Kintsugi highlights them, filling them with gold so that the very places of damage become the most valuable parts of the piece. The same is true for you. Your cracks are not signs of failure—they are the places where your strength becomes visible. The seasons that broke you were never meant to disqualify you; they were designed to distinguish you. Your heartbreaks, your disappointments, your financial strain, your academic pressure, your identity crises—none of it was wasted. These are the very spaces where God pours His grace, His power, and His presence, turning what once felt like weakness into undeniable evidence of transformation. Your story is not powerful in spite of what you've been through—it is powerful because of it. Your resilience is not hidden in perfection; it is revealed in the places where you were rebuilt. And when others look at your life, they won't just see where you were broken—they will see how you were restored, strengthened, and made whole in a way only God could orchestrate.

Choosing the Bounce-Forward

Resilience is not about bouncing back—it is about bouncing forward. It is not a return to who you were before the storm; it is a transformation into someone wiser, stronger, and more self-aware because of it. The goal is not restoration to your old self, but elevation into your next self. Just like a rubber ball rises highest after it hits the ground with force, the pressure of your challenges has the potential to propel you upward in ways comfort never could. But that upward movement is not automatic—it is intentional. It requires a mindset that refuses to stay defeated and a faith that remains anchored even when everything around you feels uncertain. Your setbacks are not meant to settle you; they are meant to strengthen you. And when you allow what tried to break you to instead build you, you discover that the very ground you hit was not your end—it was the force that launched you into who you were always becoming.

Hope as Your Anchor

Every resilient person has an anchor—something that holds them steady when life becomes unsteady. It may be your faith, your sense of purpose, your family, or the vision God has placed deep within your spirit. Whatever it is, that anchor becomes the difference between being carried by the storm and being shaped through it. Without an anchor, life's pressures will toss you endlessly, leaving you reactive, unstable, and easily overwhelmed. But with an anchor, those same storms begin to work for you instead of against you, developing your strength, refining your perspective, and deepening your trust. Your anchor does not remove the storm—it stabilizes you within it. And when optimism, growth, and resilience come together, they do more than sustain you—they prepare you. They position you to not just survive what you've been through, but to step into what's ahead with clarity, strength, and readiness. Because what's next for you is not just survival—it is abundance. And now, you're ready to step into it.

When Spring Hands You to Summer

As you step out of this chapter, picture yourself as the earth after a warm spring rain—softened, renewed, and quietly alive with possibility. The seeds you planted in faith, even when you could not see immediate results, are beginning to respond beneath the surface. Roots are stretching deeper, anchoring you in ways that will sustain what is coming next. The first signs of green are breaking through the soil, subtle but undeniable, revealing that something is growing even if it is not yet fully formed. And while everything may not be complete, the beginnings are real. You are not defined by the barren seasons you endured. You are not behind, no matter how it may have felt. You are not forgotten, even in the moments when it seemed silent. You are not too late—your timing is still within God's design. You are a seed awakening, coming into life at the exact moment you were meant to. And as spring gives way to summer, the soil of your life is no longer prepared just for survival—it is ready for flourishing. What comes next will not be small, it will not be fragile, and it will not be accidental. It will be the result of everything that has been forming within you. What comes next is abundance.

Chapter 3: Summer Success: Navigating Growth and Opportunities

When the Sun Reveals What You've Planted

Summer is the season when life exposes everything you've been cultivating — intentionally or accidentally. The seeds you planted in spring, whether rooted in optimism, discipline, fear, or avoidance, begin pushing through the soil of your reality. Some appear as open doors. Some emerge as opportunities you prayed for. Others reveal gaps you didn't realize existed. But summer always exposes truth. It is the season that refuses to let potential stay hidden. Suddenly life feels alive. Movement accelerates. Possibility expands. Favor seems to chase you. And for many people, this is both exhilarating and overwhelming. Because growth isn't just a blessing — it is a responsibility, a weight, and a mirror. Many pray for abundance, but abundance demands that you become the kind of person who can sustain what you asked for. Summer brings you into that tension. It teaches you that favor requires maturity, opportunity requires readiness, and success requires a level of discipline most people never develop. God doesn't bless you simply to bask in the light; He blesses you to multiply that light, to steward it well, and to become someone who can carry the expansion without collapsing beneath it. Summer is loud, bright, urgent, and demanding — but if you learn to navigate it with wisdom and faith, it becomes the season that launches you into your next level of purpose.

Section 1: Seizing Opportunities for Personal and Professional Growth

When Opportunity Knocks Before You're Ready

Growth rarely enters your life politely. Opportunity doesn't knock softly; it kicks the door open at the most inconvenient time. It shows up when your confidence is shaky, when you're questioning your abilities, when imposter syndrome is screaming the loudest. And yet, those are the exact moments when opportunity is most divine. God rarely aligns openings with your comfort level; He aligns them with your calling. That's why so many people miss their season—not because they weren't gifted, but because they were waiting to feel ready. And readiness is a myth. Opportunities demand courage before competence. They require movement before mastery. They rarely arrive wrapped in clarity, and almost never when you feel secure. In fact, growth often hides inside the very things you're afraid to attempt: the job you think you're underqualified for, the project that stretches your limits, the relationship that exposes your vulnerability, the divine nudge that disrupts your normal routines. If you only move when you're comfortable, you will never move when it matters. The truth is this: *Most opportunities don't disappear—they expire.* They have windows, not waiting rooms. And too many people stand at the window of destiny, watching it close, whispering "maybe next time," unaware that next time rarely looks the same. Opportunity doesn't slow down for hesitation, fear, or indecision. God doesn't pause your calling until your self-esteem catches up. He invites you into the risk because He knows what's on the other side of it. This first subsection is your wake-up call: You cannot pray for a season of abundance while refusing the discomfort of elevation. Growth is always inconvenient, always stretching, always demanding more than the bare minimum. But the moment you say "yes"—even trembling—the entire trajectory of your life begins to shift. You don't wait for bravery; you build it in motion.

Why Opportunity Often Feels Like Fear

Fear is not a sign that you're unqualified—it is a signal that you are standing at the edge of growth, right where your next level is trying to pull you forward. Every meaningful opportunity carries a level of uncertainty, often presenting itself like a shadowed doorway where you cannot see what's inside until you choose to step through it. And yes, that step will feel uncomfortable. It will challenge your confidence, stretch your capacity, and confront every excuse that tells you to stay where you are. But discomfort is not danger—it is development. Courage, in these moments, becomes more valuable than credentials, because it is not the most prepared who move forward—it is the most willing. Movement matters more than mastery, because you refine your skill in motion, not in hesitation. And destiny will always demand more from you than your desire to stay safe. Fear is not your enemy—it is often the doorway. Stagnation is the real threat, because it convinces you to stay where growth can no longer reach you.

The Real-World Analogy: The Internship Window

Imagine this: It's sophomore year. Summer internships open, and applications flood the system. Some students apply immediately—not because they're the most confident, but because they understand timing. Others procrastinate, convincing themselves that they'll apply once they feel more prepared, more polished, more "put together." But the deadline comes. The window closes. And those who hesitated spend the rest of the semester telling themselves, "Next year will be my year," not realizing that momentum isn't promised—timing is. Life is full of internship windows. Moments where things open briefly—relationships, opportunities, leadership roles, creative inspirations, divine assignments. These windows don't wait for your courage. They don't broaden because you're second-guessing yourself. They open, and they close. And the ones who advance are not always the most talented—they're the ones who moved when the window was cracked open. Your twenties, thirties, forties—every decade has windows. Summers of opportunity appear, and whether you step through determines how your story unfolds. The world may reward credentials, but destiny rewards courage. When the window opens, your responsibility is simple: apply.

Preparing for the Yes Before It Arrives

Preparation is the secret weapon of every successful season. Opportunity may arrive suddenly, but your readiness is built long before the door opens. Too many people pray for abundance but refuse to cultivate the discipline that abundance requires. They want the platform without the preparation, the influence without the integrity, the harvest without the hard work. But summer doesn't bless laziness—it blesses alignment. Preparation looks like studying when no one is asking you to. Practicing when no one is watching. Budgeting when your income still feels small. Honing your craft when no compliments are coming. Saying "no" to distractions because your "yes" has purpose. Preparation is not glamorous; it is gritty. It's waking up early, staying up late, stretching your abilities, and investing in the future you want—not the one you're settling for. But preparation is also spiritual. It's aligning your heart with God's pace. It's learning discernment so you can identify which opportunities are divine and which are distractions. It's healing emotional wounds so you don't sabotage blessings. It's building the character to support the calling you're praying for. Preparation plants roots deep enough to sustain growth when success arrives.

What This Season Is Asking of You

Summer asks one question: *Will you steward the opportunity I've given you?* Not admire it. Not brag about it. Steward it. You are standing in a season that requires boldness, readiness, and trust. This is your time to recognize doors when they appear, to move even when you're trembling, and to prepare even when no audience is watching. Growth is not accidental. It is intentional. And summer reveals who has been preparing in the dark.

Section 2: Strategies for Maximizing Success During Peak Times

When Blessing Becomes Both Gift and Weight

Summer teaches you a lesson that every successful person eventually learns: Blessing comes with responsibility. When life heats up—when opportunities multiply and momentum accelerates—most people assume the hardest part is over. They think the challenge was getting the door to open. But the truth is, opening the door is only Act One. Carrying what's on the other side is the real test. Success exposes you. It magnifies everything—your strengths, your habits, your insecurities, your discipline, your distractions. It forces you to level up or fall apart. Growth doesn't just give you more—it requires more. More focus. More boundaries. More maturity. More humility. More stewardship. When God elevates you, the spotlight that shines on your gift also shines on your gaps. The very season you prayed for becomes the season that demands your highest version. Summer is warm, yes, but it's also intense. The very heat that makes things flourish is the same heat that can cause things to burn if you're not intentional. That's why success feels heavy sometimes. Not because you're unqualified—but because you're growing into the capacity that abundance requires. God never gives blessing without giving responsibility. Summer is not just a reward—it's an invitation to steward your life with strategy, wisdom, and purpose, because unmanaged success is just delayed failure.

Why Success Needs Structure

Here's the uncomfortable truth: *Success without structure collapses.*
It doesn't matter how gifted, charismatic, or passionate a person is—if they lack system, success will exhaust them. If they lack boundaries, opportunities will overwhelm them. If they lack discipline, momentum will slip through their fingers like sand.

Think about athletes. Winning one championship takes talent. Maintaining a dynasty takes structure. Think about entrepreneurs. Launching a business takes courage. Sustaining one takes order. Think about creatives. Going viral takes timing. Staying relevant takes consistency. Structure is not restrictive—it is protective. It ensures you don't lose what you've worked so hard to gain. You cannot build a skyscraper on an unstable foundation. You cannot sustain momentum with a chaotic mind. You cannot manage growth with the same habits you had when life was smaller. Success expands your territory. Structure strengthens your stewardship. Without both, you shine briefly—and burn quickly. The reason most people collapse in their season of abundance isn't because they were unprepared for success, but because they were unprepared for the *maintenance* of success. Growth demands order. Summer requires systems. Blessings need boundaries. If you want longevity, you must build structures that honor your future, not just your present.

The Real-World Analogy: Finals Week Focus

Think about finals week in college. It's exhausting, overwhelming, and intense — the kind of pressure that exposes how prepared you really are. Sleep is scarce. Expectations are high. Every decision feels amplified. Yet somehow, it's also where some of the greatest breakthroughs happen. Not because the material is easier, but because focus becomes non-negotiable. The students who thrive during finals week aren't always the smartest in the room. They're the ones who manage their time intentionally, pace their energy wisely, and stay disciplined even when stress is at its peak. They understand that pressure doesn't require panic — it requires structure. Success works the same way. You can drown in its demands, or you can rise through its intensity. The difference isn't talent. It's stewardship.

Keys to Maximizing Peak Times

1. **Prioritize What Moves Purpose Forward**
    a. Being busy is not the same as being effective. Summer seasons throw tasks at you, but only a few truly matter. Ask: *"Is this helping me grow or just keeping me occupied?"*
2. **Create Rhythms, Not Just Routines**
    a. Schedules keep you organized. Rhythms keep you alive. Prayer, rest, health, reflection — these sustain your momentum and protect you from burnout.
3. Build Accountability Into Your Circle

a. Success has blind spots. You need people who check your ego, guard your perspective, challenge your decisions, and remind you who you are. Your circle becomes your ceiling — or your springboard.

What Summer Teaches Your Soul

Summer doesn't just test your talent — it tests your stewardship.
It reveals whether you know how to manage what you prayed for, not just celebrate it. Talent may open the door, but stewardship determines how long you're allowed to stay in the room. Success exposes your habits, your discipline, and your maturity under pressure. Success is not simply about seizing opportunities; it is about sustaining them with wisdom. It's about knowing when to push and when to pause, when to expand and when to protect what you've already built. Without wisdom, momentum becomes reckless — impressive for a moment, but unsustainable over time. But even with strong strategy, one truth remains: Success is not permanent. Seasons shift. What worked before may not work forever, and what once felt effortless may require intention in the next phase. So the real question becomes this: How do you maintain momentum when the winds change?

Section 3: Sustaining Momentum in the Midst of Change

When Progress Requires Continuous Movement

Momentum dies the moment you stop moving. Not because you failed — but because you paused too long waiting to feel ready again. Life won't always wait for your confidence to return. Opportunities evolve. Seasons shift. Momentum requires motion — even when the direction changes. Your task in summer is not just to grow. It is to keep growing, even as the season transforms.

When the Winds Shift

Every season of success eventually slows. The applause quiets. The pace changes. What once felt effortless begins to feel unfamiliar. Many panic here — not because they lost ability, but because they mistook momentum for permanence. A slowing pace is not a setback. It is a signal that your season is shifting. The road ahead may curve like a mountain path — forcing you to slow down, not because you're failing, but because you're climbing.

The Real-World Analogy: Virality and Sarah Jakes Roberts

In a generation raised online, momentum is often confused with attention. You post one video — it goes viral. Two weeks later — engagement drops. Fear kicks in: *"Did I fall off?"* No — you just met the natural rhythm of growth. Momentum is wave-like. Look at **Sarah Jakes Roberts**. Her influence did not explode overnight. It grew through consistency in the quiet seasons — serving, preaching, writing, studying, preparing long before anyone filled an arena. Momentum is not built in moments of applause. It is built in the moments when no one is watching. Consistency beats virality every time.

Principles for Sustaining Momentum

1. **Stay Rooted, Not Rushed**
   a. Growth often tempts you to rush — to stack more, post more, do more. But lasting success comes from being rooted, not reactive. The deeper your roots (discipline, faith, self-awareness), the less likely you'll be uprooted by a season of change.
2. **Revisit Your 'Why' Regularly**
   a. When momentum slows, it's easy to lose sight of purpose. Go back to the reason you started. Write it down, speak it aloud, and remind yourself that impact isn't measured in speed, but in consistency.
3. **Redefine Progress**
   a. Sometimes progress isn't about doing more — it's about maintaining peace while doing less. The shift from movement to maintenance is still growth. It's maturity.

The Rhythm of Rising

Momentum is not constant. It pulses. It breathes. It rises and falls like a heartbeat — steady, alive, and necessary. True growth isn't about staying at the top of the wave, chasing highs, or forcing perpetual acceleration. It's about learning how to move with wisdom when the tide shifts — adjusting your pace without losing your direction, staying faithful even when the surge slows. Momentum isn't lost when things quiet down; it's refined. The seasons that feel slower are often the ones teaching you how to sustain progress without adrenaline, applause, or urgency driving every step. And as summer begins to fade, life gently invites you into its next holy season: **Reflection. Release. Renewal.**

The Heat That Reveals Your Strength

Summer is a beautiful paradox — abundant yet demanding, bright yet exhausting, full yet stretching. You've learned how to seize opportunities, maximize success, and sustain momentum even as life shifts around you. But all seasons come to a close. The sun eventually sets, and the warmth begins to soften. And when it does, something sacred happens: You become aware of what needs reflection. What needs release. What needs refining before you can grow again. Growth doesn't reach maturity in the heat alone — it matures in the reflection that follows. Summer prepares you for harvest. But autumn teaches you how to carry it well. As you step out of summer's light and into autumn's quiet, take a moment to ask yourself: *"What have I gained? And what am I willing to release so I can grow deeper?"* Autumn is the sacred pause — the season where God asks you to reflect, release, and realign. What you learned in summer will guide you, but what you release in autumn will free you. Turn the page. The leaves are beginning to fall. And clarity is calling your name.

Chapter 4: Autumn Reflections: Learning and Letting Go

The Season That Reveals What You Must Release

The truth is this: you cannot grow into what God has for you while clinging to what He is calling you away from. Autumn is a season of sacred pause — a divine invitation to slow down, look back, and discern the lessons woven into your life's story. Just as trees release their leaves, you too are invited to release what no longer serves your spirit. Reflection is not regret — it is revelation. It is the clarity that emerges when God allows the dust of your past to settle so you can finally see His fingerprints on the road behind you. This chapter will guide you through the holy work of reflection, the courage of release, and the wisdom extracted from every battle you've survived. Autumn is the season when God prepares you for your next elevation by revealing what must fall away. Let's step into the quiet, into the clarity, into the courage of autumn.

Section 1: Reflecting on Past Experiences

When God Says, "Look Again"

You cannot move forward with clarity until you are willing to look back with honesty. Reflection is not about rewinding time or reliving every painful moment—it is about revealing truth, about seeing with spiritual eyes what you could not fully understand while you were in it. God often whispers His greatest lessons after the storm, not during it. When you are fighting just to survive, your vision is clouded, your emotions are heightened, and your focus is limited to making it through the moment. But when the winds settle and the noise quiets, when the leaves begin to fall and life slows just enough for you to breathe again, God gently invites you, *"Now, look again."* Autumn becomes that sacred pause between what was and what will be—a holy space where reflection is not meant to shame you, but to shape you. It is where God meets you in the quiet corners of your memory, illuminating patterns, revealing lessons, and bringing clarity to moments that once felt confusing or painful. Your past does not need to be relived—it needs to be understood. Because when you understand it, you stop being controlled by it, and you start being refined through it.

The Mirror That Reveals More Than Your Reflection

Reflection is like standing before a mirror that doesn't just show your face—it reveals your faith. It allows you to see beyond the surface of what happened and into the deeper meaning of why it happened. What once felt like detours begin to reveal themselves as divine direction points when viewed through spiritual hindsight. What once felt like loss starts to look like protection, and what once felt like silence begins to sound like strategy. In reflection, you realize that God was not absent—He was intentional, working behind the scenes in ways you could not yet understand. But reflection requires stillness, and stillness requires surrender. You cannot rush clarity, and you cannot force revelation. You have to be willing to pause, to sit with what was, and to trust that God will meet you there with understanding. And surrender demands trust—the kind of trust that believes God was present even when it didn't feel like it. Growth does not come from obsessing over what happened or replaying every detail in frustration; it comes when you shift your posture and ask, *"God, what were You showing me through this?"* Because in that question, you move from confusion to clarity, and from pain to purpose.

When Patterns Become Revelation

Every season leaves clues about the next one, because God rarely wastes experiences—He repurposes them. Nothing you've walked through was meaningless, even if it felt confusing at the time. But if you never pause long enough to reflect, you risk repeating lessons you were meant to graduate from. Growth is not just about going through seasons—it's about learning from them. Just like Israel wandering in the wilderness, you can witness miracles and still miss the message if you refuse to slow down. What should take days can stretch into years when reflection is ignored, not because God is withholding progress, but because you are overlooking the instruction. Reflection has a way of bringing hidden patterns into the light. It reveals cycles you must break, wounds you must stop reopening, growth you need to acknowledge, and wisdom you are meant to carry forward into your next season. It helps you see where you've been stuck, where you've been healed, and where God has been faithful even when you didn't recognize it. Your wilderness was never meant to destroy you—it was designed to develop you. It was preparation, not punishment, shaping you into someone ready to carry what comes next.

When Pain Becomes a Prophet

When reflection is guided by faith, even pain begins to preach. What once felt like something you needed to escape becomes something that carries a message you cannot afford to ignore. The heartbreak you endured may have been teaching you the difference between attachment and alignment—showing you that not everything you feel deeply is meant to stay. The delay you resented may have been introducing you to divine pacing, teaching you that God's timing is not slow—it is strategic. The disappointment that shook you may have been revealing a deeper level of resilience within you, proving that you are stronger than the moment that tried to break you. Pain becomes prophetic when you allow it to instruct you instead of intimidate you, when you stop running from it and start listening to what it is trying to say. You don't reflect to relive the pain or reopen old wounds—you reflect to redeem it, to extract the wisdom hidden inside it, and to carry that insight forward so that what once hurt you now helps you.

What Autumn Teaches Through Quiet Eyes

Reflection doesn't change your past—it clarifies it. It doesn't rewrite what happened, but it reshapes how you understand it. When you look back through God's lens, you begin to see that nothing was wasted. Every tear becomes a seed of insight, carrying lessons you could not have learned any other way. Every closed door reveals itself as a chapter of divine protection, guarding you from spaces that were never meant to sustain you. Every storm becomes a teacher, training your discernment, strengthening your faith, and preparing you for what lies ahead. In reflection, you begin to recognize that God was present in every moment—even the ones that felt silent, confusing, or painful. And once you've gathered what He revealed, once you've allowed clarity to replace confusion and wisdom to replace regret, your next step becomes undeniable. Because clarity always leads to a call. And that call is this: *Release what no longer belongs.*

Section 2: The Art of Letting Go and Releasing What No Longer Serves

When Holding On Becomes the Weight

You cannot step into your next season while dragging the remains of your last one. What you refuse to release will eventually restrict where you can go. Growth demands movement, and movement requires open hands. Letting go is not weakness — it is spiritual warfare. It is choosing obedience over attachment. Peace over pride. Freedom over familiarity. God cannot pour new oil into vessels still filled with yesterday's residue. New assignments require clean space. Fresh vision needs room to breathe. What once sustained you can now contaminate what God is trying to produce next. Some things in your life have expired, yet you continue to hold them close — not because they are life-giving, but because they are familiar. Familiar pain feels safer than unfamiliar freedom. Old patterns feel easier than new responsibility. But familiarity is not the same as alignment. And what once fit you can become the very thing that limits you.

The Weight You Were Never Meant to Carry

Much of the heaviness you feel is not coming from your current season—it is coming from what you refuse to release. You are not just carrying today's responsibilities; you are dragging yesterday's weight into a space that was never designed to hold it. Old mindsets that no longer align with who you are becoming. Expired relationships that have already served their purpose. Guilt tied to who you used to be, even though God has already called you forward. Dreams that once fit your life but no longer match your current calling. Bitterness that disguises itself as boundaries, convincing you that holding on is protecting you when it is actually preventing you. When you try to move forward with your hands full of the past, you will always find yourself exhausted, breathless, and unable to run with clarity. And here is the divine truth: God prunes what He plans to multiply. He removes not to punish, but to prepare. Even the branches that are still producing must be cut back so they can bear greater fruit. What feels like loss is often divine intention, making room for a level of growth your current weight cannot sustain.

When Holding On Hurts More Than Healing Does

There comes a moment when your grip becomes the very thing breaking you, when what you are holding onto begins to hold you back. You say you want peace—but do you want it more than you want control? You say you trust God—but do you trust Him enough to release what He has already removed? These are the questions that reveal where your faith is still being formed. Because release is not a one-time decision; it is a repeated discipline. It is the daily, sometimes moment-by-moment choice to let go of what your flesh wants to cling to. You may find yourself releasing the same memory, the same fear, the same person, the same identity—again and again—until your heart finally aligns with your spirit and your obedience catches up with God's instruction. Letting go is not always immediate, but it is intentional. And the longer you resist it, the heavier it becomes. Healing does not begin when the pain disappears—it begins when the grip loosens. Because healing always starts where holding on ends.

The Holy Exchange of Release

Whenever God asks you to let go, He is not abandoning you—He is advancing you. Heaven never empties a life without intention. God does not remove without replacement; He clears space so glory can enter. He is making room—room for a new calling that fits who you are becoming, room for relationships aligned with your assignment, room for wisdom that can only be carried by a surrendered heart, and room for versions of yourself that could not emerge while your hands were full. Release is the divine exchange, where the lesser leaves so the greater can arrive. It is the sacred transaction where obedience unlocks abundance. Abraham had to release Ishmael to establish Isaac—because promise could not coexist with compromise. Ruth had to release Moab to step into destiny—because loyalty to the past could not follow her into purpose. Jesus had to release His life to receive His crown—because sacrifice became the doorway to resurrection. What you release ultimately reveals what you believe about God. If you trust Him, you open your hands; if you fear loss, you tighten your grip. But hear this clearly: God never asks for release without resurrection on the other side.

The Freedom Found in Open Hands

Letting go doesn't mean you stop caring — it means you stop carrying what was never meant to stay in your hands forever. You can honor what was while still releasing its weight. Care remembers; carrying exhausts. Letting go is an act of trust. It is believing that God's removal is never random and His pruning is never cruel. What He lifts from your life is always connected to what He is preparing to grow within it. Renewal often begins with subtraction, not addition. And now that your hands are free — no longer clenched around what has passed — you are positioned for the final work of autumn. Not rushing ahead. Not numbing the past. But extracting wisdom from what remains. Because what you learn from this season will determine how well you walk into the next.

Section 3: Extracting Wisdom from Challenges

When Pain Becomes Strategy

Pain without reflection is just suffering—it lingers without purpose, weighs you down without producing anything meaningful, and leaves you carrying experiences you were never meant to simply endure. But pain with revelation becomes strategy. It becomes instruction. It becomes insight that equips you for what's next. Every challenge you've survived carries within it a form of divine wisdom, waiting to be uncovered. The heartbreak you endured, the disappointment that shook you, the betrayal that caught you off guard, the delay that tested your patience—none of it was wasted. There was something in each of those moments that was shaping your perspective, sharpening your discernment, and strengthening your capacity. But many people move through pain too quickly, eager to escape the discomfort, and in doing so, they leave behind the very wisdom that pain was trying to give them. They graduate from the experience, but they never collect the lesson. And because of that, they find themselves repeating cycles instead of rising from them. But when you slow down long enough to ask what your pain was teaching you, everything changes. You stop seeing your experiences as random hardship and start recognizing them as intentional preparation. Because the truth is this: God never wastes a wound. What hurt you was also shaping you, and when you extract the wisdom from it, you ensure that what once broke you now builds you.

The Lessons Hidden in Loss

Wisdom does not always arrive wrapped in victory or celebration; often, it is hidden in the rubble of what collapsed. It is uncovered in the moments that felt confusing, painful, and unresolved. Scripture shows us this clearly through Joseph's journey—every betrayal by his brothers, every moment in the pit, every false accusation, and every prison cell was not detouring him from his destiny, but developing him for the throne he could not yet see. What looked like delay was actually preparation, and what felt like injustice was shaping his capacity to lead. The same is true for you. Your suffering was not senseless, your struggles were not empty, and your battles were not meaningless interruptions. They were classrooms—spaces where your character was refined, your perspective was sharpened, and your strength was built. The lessons may not have been obvious while you were in the middle of it, but they were there, forming something within you that comfort never could. So before you curse the season that broke you, pause long enough to ask what it was trying to teach you. Because within that question is the key to turning your pain into wisdom and your experience into preparation for what comes next.

When Maturity Rewrites Your Perspective

Spiritual maturity does not always change your circumstances, but it will always change your questions. You stop praying only for escape and begin praying for understanding, recognizing that what you are going through may be shaping something greater than what you are trying to avoid. You begin to see God's "no" not as rejection, but as His "not yet," trusting that His timing carries wisdom you may not yet understand. What once felt like rejection starts to reveal itself as redirection, guiding you away from spaces that could not sustain your growth and toward places aligned with your purpose. Over time, you realize that your testimony is not built from your victories alone, but from the very things that once terrified you—the moments that stretched your faith, challenged your identity, and forced you to depend on God in deeper ways. Mature believers do not run from pain or pretend it doesn't exist; they mine it. They are willing to dig through the dirt of their experiences, searching for the gold God intentionally placed there. Because they understand that buried within every difficult season is a revelation, and when that revelation is uncovered, it transforms not only how they see their past, but how they walk into their future.

Purpose Revealed in the Pattern

Wisdom often reveals itself only when you learn to zoom out, stepping back far enough to see the full picture God has been painting all along. In the moment, experiences can feel random, frustrating, or even insignificant, but with perspective, patterns begin to emerge. David did not become a warrior in the palace—he became one in the pasture, in the quiet, unseen places where no one was watching and no applause was given. The lion and the bear were not interruptions; they were preparation for the Goliath he did not yet know he would face. What felt small was actually strategic. And your life has worked the same way. Every disappointment has been training your resilience. Every delay has been preparing your patience. Every detour has been directing your steps toward something more aligned than what you originally planned. Nothing was random, and nothing was wasted. The process that stretched you is the same process that strengthened you. So instead of resenting what you went through, learn to respect it—because it forged a version of you capable of carrying what comes next.

The Wisdom Autumn Hands You

Wisdom is not found in avoidance—it is found in awareness. It is not gained by running from difficulty, but by leaning into it long enough to understand what it was trying to teach you. Every challenge you have faced has added something sacred to your story, even if you did not recognize it at the time. The moments that stretched you expanded your capacity. The seasons that confused you sharpened your discernment. The experiences that hurt you deepened your perspective and strengthened your faith. Nothing you walked through was empty; it was all contributing to who you are becoming. And when you choose to carry that wisdom with you into your next season—when you allow what you've learned to inform how you move, how you choose, and how you trust—you begin to operate differently. You no longer approach life from a place of fear or uncertainty, but from a place of clarity and growth. And in that shift, you discover that you are no longer just surviving transitions—*you thrive through them.*

When the Trees Stand Bare but Not Broken

As autumn ends, the trees stand bare—yet not defeated. Their branches are empty, but not abandoned, and their roots remain deep, quietly preparing for what comes next. So it is with you. You have reflected, released, and redeemed your past with honesty and faith. You have discovered wisdom where there once was pain, clarity where there once was confusion, and strength where there once was fear. Now you stand ready—bare, but not broken; still, but not stagnant; lightened, but not lost. Autumn has done its holy work, teaching you how to reflect, release, and gather what truly matters. But every season eventually turns cold, and even the strongest faith will face winter winds. In the next chapter, you will learn how to stand strong when life freezes over—how to endure, how to trust, and how to find God in the coldest days of your journey. Turn the page. Winter is coming—but so is your resilience.

Chapter 5: Winter Resilience: Facing Challenges with Strength

When Cold Seasons Reveal Who You Really Are

Hardship is not optional; it is inevitable. The cold of winter comes for every soul — through loss, disappointment, unexpected trials, or silent seasons where nothing seems to move. Winter strips away comfort, exposes truth, and brings you face-to-face with the strength (or fragility) of your foundation. But here is the revelation: Winter is not sent to weaken you. Winter is sent to reveal you. It exposes what was never solid, highlights what needs strengthening, and pushes you to build resilience in places you once neglected. Winter is the season where God calls you to endure, to trust, to learn, and to grow even when the path feels frozen beneath your feet. Resilience is not about avoiding struggle — it's about cultivating unwavering faith in the middle of it. This chapter will show you how to stand firm when life becomes relentless, how to equip yourself spiritually and mentally for difficult seasons, and how to maintain hope when the world around you feels cold and silent. Winter isn't just a season to survive — it's a season to *become strong.*

Section 1: Building Resilience During Tough Times

When Adversity Enters Without Knocking

Adversity doesn't knock politely—it barges in without warning, disrupting your rhythm and demanding your attention whether you feel ready or not. Dreams begin to freeze, plans stall in place, relationships shift in unexpected ways, and progress that once felt steady suddenly slows to a crawl. What used to feel manageable now feels heavy, and every step forward requires more effort than the last. Winter seasons do not ask for permission; they arrive with force, unapologetically confronting the strength of your foundation. But hear this clearly: true resilience is not built in comfort—it is forged in the cold. It develops in the quiet moments where no one is watching, where your faith is tested and your endurance is stretched. It grows in silence, strengthens in hardship, and matures in those moments when giving up feels easier than pressing on.

Winter does not come to crush you—it comes to carve you, shaping your character, refining your perspective, and building a strength within you that ease could never produce.

Roots That Strengthen Beneath the Frozen Ground

Resilience begins in your heart and mind long before it is ever visible in your actions. It is cultivated intentionally—through the perspective you choose, the faith you hold onto, and the disciplined decisions you make when life feels uncertain. Winter is not punishment; it is preparation, even when it does not feel like it. Like a tree standing bare, exposed, and vulnerable against the cold, there is a deeper work happening beneath the surface that cannot be seen at first glance. Beneath the icy soil, its roots are strengthening, deepening, and anchoring themselves in ways that will sustain future growth. Your soul does the same in winter seasons. What looks like stagnation on the surface is actually internal development—the kind that builds endurance, strengthens your identity, and prepares you to carry the weight of what is coming next. You may not feel like you are moving forward, but something within you is being fortified. Progress is not always visible, but it is always happening, shaping you quietly for the moment when growth will once again rise to the surface.

Anchoring Yourself in God When the Season Feels Silent

Resilience isn't only mental toughness—it is spiritual grounding, the kind that anchors you when everything around you feels uncertain. It is not just about pushing through; it is about staying rooted. Prayer becomes your reminder that storms have limits, that nothing you face is without boundary or end. Scripture becomes your reassurance that every season carries purpose, even when you cannot immediately see it. And God's presence becomes your greatest comfort, reminding you that you are never walking through any season alone. As Isaiah 40:31 declares, *"Those who hope in the Lord will renew their strength,"* and that renewal is not just physical—it is spiritual, emotional, and deeply internal. Winter seasons test your hope, stretching it beyond surface-level belief into something deeper and more resilient. Yet in that testing, your hope is also refined. Every unanswered prayer becomes an invitation to trust God beyond what you can see. Every delay becomes an opportunity for spiritual strengthening. Every quiet moment becomes a sacred space where God whispers, "Stay with Me." And it is in these very moments—when life feels still, silent, and uncertain—that your faith is no longer fragile but forged. Winter is where your faith becomes unshakeable, not because the storm never came, but because you learned how to stand in it.

Real-World Imagery of Winter Strength

Winter is a forge, shaping your inner steel in ways comfort never could. It is the quiet, intense pressure that refines who you are beneath the surface, strengthening your character where no one else can see. Winter is a river under ice—still moving, still progressing, even when everything on the surface appears frozen and unchanged. It is night before dawn, a deep and stretching darkness that is not meant to consume you, but to prepare the horizon for a sunrise you cannot yet see. Winter does not stop life; it slows it just enough for you to strengthen, to recalibrate, and to become more rooted than you were before. In these slower, colder seasons, distractions fade and what truly matters becomes clear. Your greatest endurance is not built in ease, but in the months that feel the coldest—when you choose to keep going, to keep trusting, and to keep believing even when nothing around you seems to be moving.

What Winter Is Strengthening Within You

Winter builds resilience not through ease, but through endurance—the kind that is developed when you choose to keep going even when everything in you wants to stop. It is in these moments of pressure and persistence that your foundation is strengthened in ways comfort could never accomplish. The more you trust God in adversity, the more rooted you become, and the less easily you are shaken by what once would have broken you. What feels like frostbite—sharp, uncomfortable, and even painful—is often the shaping hand of your Creator, refining your character and preparing you for the increase that spring will bring. Nothing you are experiencing is without purpose; it is all building capacity within you. And now that you have begun to understand resilience at a heart-level, the next step is just as important. Because strength alone is not enough—you must also learn how to navigate hardship with wisdom, intention, and strategy, not fear.

Section 2: Strategies for Navigating Hardships

When the Storm Becomes Your Training Ground

Hardship isn't a test you can skip—it's a training ground ordained for your growth, whether you feel ready for it or not. Life will not pause for your comfort, and storms will not wait for your convenience. Challenges will come with force, knocking the wind out of you and demanding more than you believe you have to give. They will stretch your patience, test your faith, and expose every area where you are not as strong as you thought. But here is the truth you cannot afford to ignore: resilience is not built by avoiding storms—it is built by walking through them with intention. You do not grow by escaping pressure; you grow by enduring it with purpose. Survival is not passive, and it is certainly not accidental—it is strategic. It requires awareness, discipline, and the willingness to move forward even when the path is unclear, trusting that every step you take in the storm is strengthening you for what comes next.

Break Down What Feels Impossible

Winter problems often look like massive, unscalable walls—intimidating, overwhelming, and impossible to move all at once. When you focus on the full weight of the situation, it can feel paralyzing, like there is no clear way forward. But what feels immovable begins to shift when you change how you approach it. Walls become manageable when you break them down into bricks—when you stop trying to conquer everything at once and instead focus on what is right in front of you. Handle today's step with intention and presence, giving your best to what is within your reach. Trust God with tomorrow's challenge, releasing the pressure to control what has not yet arrived. Stop trying to solve the entire mountain in one moment and instead commit to steady, faithful movement. Because in seasons like this, progress is not about speed—it is about consistency. And it is through small, daily acts of obedience that big breakthroughs are quietly built over time.

Anchor Yourself in Faith and Community

You were not created to endure winter alone, no matter how strong or independent you believe yourself to be. Seasons of hardship are not meant to be carried in isolation; they are meant to be navigated with support, both spiritual and relational. Daily prayer keeps your spirit steady, anchoring you when your emotions feel unstable and your circumstances feel uncertain. Scripture keeps your perspective aligned, reminding you of truth when your thoughts begin to drift toward fear or doubt. Mentors and trusted friends keep your heart encouraged, offering wisdom, accountability, and presence when you need it most. As Proverbs 27:17 reminds us, *"Iron sharpens iron,"* and growth often happens in the friction of honest, supportive relationships. Isolation only intensifies the cold of winter, making challenges feel heavier than they truly are. But community—intentional, faith-filled, and consistent—has the power to make even the hardest seasons not only bearable, but survivable.

Maintain a Perspective That Outlasts the Storm

Hardship is temporary, even when it feels like it will last forever, but God's promises are eternal and unchanging regardless of what you are facing in the moment. Winter is part of the cycle—it is a necessary season, not the conclusion of your story—and what feels like an ending is often just a transition into something greater. There is purpose in the pressure, even when you cannot immediately see it, because pressure has a way of revealing, refining, and strengthening what is within you. Just as Paul learned in 2 Corinthians 12:9, God's strength is made perfect in weakness, meaning the very areas where you feel inadequate are often the places where His power is most clearly displayed. Your hardest moments are not random interruptions; they may be the exact spaces where God is preparing your greatest impact, building a depth within you that will one day serve others in ways you cannot yet fully understand.

The Tools Winter Places in Your Hands

Challenges will always come—there is no season of life completely untouched by pressure—but your response is what determines whether those challenges define you or refine you. You may not have control over what you face, but you do have control over how you respond, how you think, and how you choose to move through it. When you combine practical strategy with spiritual grounding, something powerful begins to happen. You are no longer simply reacting to hardship—you are navigating it with intention, clarity, and faith. You shift from merely surviving what is in front of you to actually growing through it, allowing each challenge to strengthen rather than weaken you. And once you understand this, the next step becomes clear. Because endurance alone is not enough—you must also cultivate the kind of mindset that fuels hope in the middle of the storm and sustains you when the pressure does not immediately lift.

Section 3: Maintaining a Positive Outlook in Adversity

When Mindset Becomes Your Survival Tool

Your mindset determines your survival more than your circumstances ever will, because while adversity is inevitable, despair is always a choice. You cannot always control what happens to you, but you can control how you interpret it, how you respond to it, and what you allow it to produce within you. Maintaining a positive outlook does not mean you ignore pain or pretend that hardship does not exist—it means you elevate your perspective beyond what you feel in the moment. It is the intentional decision to see God's hand at work even when the clouds refuse to part and clarity feels distant. Optimism in winter is not unrealistic or naïve; it is spiritual discernment. It is the ability to recognize that what looks like delay may actually be development, that what feels like silence may actually be strategy, and that even in the coldest seasons, God is still actively working on your behalf.

The Power of a Renewed Perspective

Positive thinking is not denial—it is alignment. It is the intentional choice to bring your perspective into agreement with truth rather than allowing your emotions to dictate your outlook. When you shift your lens, everything begins to shift with it. What once felt like a setback starts to reveal itself as a setup for something greater. Endings begin to look like openings for new opportunities. Delays take on new meaning as seasons of development, and even silence starts to feel like strategy rather than absence. This kind of perspective does not happen by accident—it requires you to retrain your mind, to discipline your thoughts, and to consistently choose to see God at work even when you cannot immediately see results. Hope begins to flourish when you learn to recognize His presence in what feels unseen and His purpose in what feels uncertain. In seasons like winter, perspective becomes your lantern—the steady light that guides you forward when everything around you feels dark, unclear, and still.

Faith-Fueled Positivity That Strengthens the Soul

Romans 8:28 reminds us that God works all things for good—even the painful things, even the confusing moments, even the seasons that seem to make no sense while you are living through them. This truth becomes the foundation for cultivating spiritual positivity, not as a surface-level mindset, but as a deeply rooted way of seeing your life through God's perspective. It begins with intentional practices that shape how you think and respond each day. Gratitude has the power to reframe your morning, shifting your focus from what is lacking to what is present. Scripture affirms your identity, reminding you of who you are when your circumstances try to tell you otherwise. Spoken truth strengthens your spirit, helping you declare what is true even when your emotions feel unstable. And quiet reflection invites God's peace, creating space for clarity, stillness, and renewal. When these practices become consistent, something begins to change within you. You realize that winter does not freeze growth—it reveals where growth truly begins, beneath the surface, in the places where God is quietly working.

Real-World Imagery of Hope in Winter

Positivity is a lantern in a blizzard—seemingly small, yet powerful enough to guide you through what feels overwhelming and disorienting. It is sunlight breaking through frost, gently warming what once felt cold, numb, and unresponsive. It is a root beneath the snow—hidden from view, yet alive, steady, and growing even when everything on the surface suggests stillness. Positivity does not always announce itself loudly; sometimes it works quietly, sustaining you in ways you do not immediately recognize. And in seasons like winter, that quiet strength becomes essential. Because hope is not weakness—it is spiritual strength. It is the decision to believe, to endure, and to trust even when circumstances try to convince you otherwise.

How Hope Changes Your Winter

Resilience without hope is endurance without joy—it may keep you moving, but it will leave you empty along the way. True resilience is not just about surviving the weight of the season; it is about carrying a sense of purpose and expectation through it. When you choose a mindset rooted in faith, something begins to shift within you. Winter is no longer a season of despair—it becomes a season of strategy, a space where God is refining your thinking, strengthening your foundation, and preparing your next move. You begin to walk with clarity instead of confusion, endure with confidence instead of fear, and survive with vision instead of uncertainty. And when that shift takes place, you are no longer just making it through—you are being transformed by it. And now, as this season comes to a close, it is time to step forward into what comes next.

The Strength Winter Leaves Behind

As winter begins to recede, it does not leave you the same—it leaves behind lessons deep enough to anchor your spirit in ways you did not have before. What you walked through was not empty; it was forming something within you. You have learned that resilience is forged in adversity, not comfort—that the very pressures you wanted to escape were the ones shaping your strength. You have discovered that practical discipline carries you through storms, sustaining you when emotions fluctuate and motivation fades. And you have come to understand that hope has the power to transform even the darkest moments into preparation for something greater. You are no longer who you were when winter began. You are wiser, stronger, more grounded, and more spiritually aware of both yourself and God's hand in your life. Winter has not weakened you—it has readied you. And now, as the season shifts, the invitation before you is different. It is not simply outward into opportunity, but inward into identity—into discovering who you are beneath everything you have endured.

Chapter 6: The Seasons of Self-Discovery: Unveiling Your True Potential

When Identity Meets Revelation

Every season you've endured has been shaping something deeper than your circumstances — it's been shaping you. Self-discovery is not a luxury; it's a divine necessity. It is the sacred work of peeling back the layers that life, pain, expectation, and survival have built — until all that remains is the truth of who God created you to be. Too often, we search for purpose in achievements, relationships, or recognition, forgetting that the greatest revelation happens within. You cannot walk confidently in your assignment until you first understand your identity. This chapter is about that unveiling — the moment when God begins to show you not just what you can do, but who you are becoming. Self-discovery is where revelation meets awareness, where faith and introspection collide, and where your life begins to look less like random events and more like divine alignment. Every strength, every weakness, every hidden talent and unexplored passion carries a clue pointing toward your purpose. But you must be willing to see yourself through God's eyes — not through failure, fear, or comparison. This is the season of becoming.

Section 1: Exploring Personal Strengths and Weaknesses

When the Mirror Reveals More Than You Expected

You cannot become who you're meant to be until you are willing to confront who you truly are, without filters, without excuses, and without avoidance. Self-discovery is not always comfortable; in fact, it often feels like standing exposed before a mirror that refuses to lie, reflecting not only your strengths but also the areas you've tried to ignore or hide. Yet this discomfort is not punishment—it is the sacred beginning of transformation. It is the moment when God begins to reveal the threads He intentionally wove into your being from the very beginning, showing you the full picture of who you are and who you are becoming. Your strengths, your weaknesses, your tendencies, and your truths are not separate pieces to be judged—they are all part of the same design. Every part of you carries meaning, and every part of you plays a role in your assignment. When you embrace that reality, you stop running from yourself and start stepping into the fullness of who God created you to be.

The Two Lenses That Shape Your Becoming

Self-discovery requires two lenses working together in harmony: divine revelation and honest reflection. Divine revelation gives you glimpses of your purpose, highlighting the gifts that continue to surface, the passions that stir your spirit, and the burdens you cannot seem to ignore no matter how hard you try. It is God gently revealing what He has placed inside of you from the beginning. Honest reflection, on the other hand, brings clarity to the areas that still need refining—your limitations, your habits, your patterns, and your vulnerabilities that may be hindering your growth. It invites you to look at yourself truthfully, not to condemn, but to develop. Your strengths begin to reveal what you are called to do, pointing you toward your assignment, while your weaknesses reveal where you must lean on God to accomplish it, reminding you that you were never meant to rely on your own strength alone. Both lenses are teachers, and both are necessary. Without revelation, you lack direction; without reflection, you lack development. But together, they guide you into a deeper understanding of who you are and who you are becoming.

When God Hides Your Strength to Grow Your Character

Sometimes your strengths feel invisible, like something you know is there but cannot quite access or express in the way you desire. You are aware of your gifts, yet they seem buried beneath seasons of waiting, uncertainty, or obscurity that make you question their impact. But hiddenness is not punishment—it is preparation. God often does His deepest work in the unseen places, shaping what He intends to reveal in the right time. Joseph's strength was hidden in a prison, where what looked like limitation was actually preparation for leadership. David's strength was hidden in a pasture, where obscurity became the training ground for kingship. Esther's strength was hidden in anonymity, where her identity was being refined before her moment of influence. God often conceals what He is cultivating, protecting it from premature exposure and allowing it to develop fully. So when your strength feels unseen, it is not because it is absent—it is because heaven is sharpening it, refining it, and preparing it for the moment it will matter most.

When Weakness Becomes a Doorway to Growth

Weakness is not meant to humiliate you—it is meant to humble you, drawing you into a deeper awareness of your need for God's strength rather than your own. As Paul wrote, "When I am weak, then I am strong," revealing the paradox that what feels like limitation is often the doorway to divine empowerment. Weakness forces you out of self-reliance and into dependency, where God's power can operate more clearly and more fully in your life. What you see as a flaw may actually be training—preparing you for compassion, humility, clarity, or leadership in ways you could not develop otherwise. Your fear may become empathy, allowing you to understand and support others with authenticity. Your insecurity may become wisdom, teaching you discernment and self-awareness. Your past failures may become your future ministry, equipping you to guide others through what you once struggled to overcome. Weakness is not a disqualifier—it is often the soil where your deepest purpose takes root and begins to grow.

What God Reveals When You Finally Stop Pretending

Self-discovery begins where denial ends, at the point where you are no longer willing to hide behind appearances or pretend to be something you are not. The moment you stop striving to appear invincible is the moment God begins shaping you with intention, working beneath the surface of your honesty. When you embrace both your beauty and your brokenness—your strengths alongside your struggles—you create space for real transformation to take place. Healing begins to unfold, clarity starts to emerge, and you gain a deeper understanding of who you truly are and who you are becoming. This kind of honesty is not weakness; it is the foundation for growth. And now that you have looked inward with truth and courage, you are ready for the next stage of the journey—uncovering the hidden gifts God has already planted within you, waiting to be revealed.

Section 2: Uncovering Hidden Talents and Passions

What's Buried in You Is Not Lost

What's hidden in you isn't missing—it's waiting for obedience to bring it alive. Every person carries dormant potential within them: gifts that have been buried by fear, dreams that have been silenced by comparison, and passions that have been overshadowed by the demands of survival. You were never created empty—you were created equipped, with intention and purpose woven into your design. But life has a way of covering what God placed within you, not to erase it, but to protect it until the right moment. Seasons of doubt, distraction, and delay can make it feel like those parts of you are gone, but they are not lost—they are waiting to be uncovered. Self-discovery is the sacred work of digging beneath the surface, uncovering what heaven has been protecting, and bringing to life what God has already placed inside of you.

Why God Conceals Before He Reveals

Before God reveals your gifts to the world, He often chooses to hide them—not as a form of punishment, but as a form of protection. What He places within you is too valuable to be exposed prematurely, so He allows it to develop in the unseen places. Hiddenness matures what is sacred, guarding it from environments that could distort or diminish its purpose. Obscurity develops your character, shaping your integrity, your discipline, and your dependence on God rather than on recognition. Quiet seasons refine your calling, helping you understand not just what you are gifted to do, but why you are called to do it. Moses' leadership was forged in the desert, long before he stood before Pharaoh. David's anointing was shaped in silence, tending sheep before leading a nation. Even Jesus spent years in preparation before stepping into three years of public ministry. Hidden seasons are not wasted—they are where God builds the depth, strength, and alignment within you that will one day become a blessing to others.

When Passion Whispers Instead of Shouts

Passion doesn't always arrive dramatically; it doesn't always come with a loud announcement or a clear, undeniable sign. Sometimes it whispers—subtle, gentle, and easy to overlook—through moments of curiosity, a sense of peace, or a creative stirring that you cannot quite explain. It reveals itself in the spaces where your soul feels awake, where time seems to move differently, and where what you are doing feels aligned with something deeper within you. But passion requires courage to follow. It often asks you to step away from what is familiar and comfortable, to release what feels safe in exchange for what feels meaningful. It demands faith, because the path it leads you on is not always clear or guaranteed. Every "yes" to passion is a "no" to settling, a decision to refuse a life that is merely convenient in favor of one that is purposeful. And every "yes" to God's stirring is a step closer to your true self—the version of you that was created to live with intention, alignment, and impact.

Real-World Analogy: The Seed Beneath the Soil

A seed buried in darkness appears lifeless, hidden beneath the surface with no visible sign of progress or potential. From the outside, it can look like nothing is happening, like growth has stalled or purpose has been delayed. But underground, something powerful is taking place. Roots are forming, stretching deeper into the soil. Strength is being developed in silence. Life is preparing itself for the moment it will break through. You are that seed. The darkness you are in is not death—it is development. It is the place where God is strengthening your foundation, shaping your capacity, and preparing you for what is to come. And when the time is right—when the growth beneath the surface is strong enough to sustain what is above it—what God planted in you will not only emerge, it will bloom with purpose, clarity, and impact.

When You Stop Chasing Visibility and Start Embracing Authenticity

Uncovering hidden talents isn't about becoming impressive—it's about becoming authentic, about aligning with who God originally created you to be rather than striving to meet external expectations. Your gifts are not random; they are God's fingerprints on your life, unique expressions of His design placed within you with intention. Your passions are not accidental; they are heaven's hints, pointing you toward the spaces where your purpose can come alive. Even your creativity carries meaning—it is part of your calling, a way God invites you to express, build, and impact the world around you. When you choose to honor what He has placed within you—rather than ignore it, compare it, or suppress it—something begins to shift. God starts aligning opportunities, connections, and moments that require exactly what you carry. What once felt hidden begins to find its place. And now, as you begin to understand what is within you, it is time to go even deeper—into how every season of your life has been shaping the person you are becoming.

Section 3: The Journey of Self-Discovery Through Life's Seasons

Every Version of You Was Needed for Who You Are Becoming

You cannot become your fullest self without walking through every season that reveals a different version of you, because each stage of life carries a unique lesson that contributes to your becoming. Self-discovery is not a single moment or a one-time realization—it is a lifelong unveiling, a continuous process of learning, growing, and understanding who you are at deeper levels. Spring awakens your dreams, reminding you of what is possible and stirring hope within you. Summer stretches your potential, challenging you to grow, to act, and to steward what has been placed in your hands. Autumn refines your wisdom, teaching you how to reflect, release, and carry forward what truly matters. Winter strengthens your resilience, building endurance and faith in the moments that feel the most difficult. Every season reveals something new about you—something necessary, something intentional—and when you embrace them all, you begin to see that none of it was wasted, and all of it was shaping you.

When God Uses Seasons as Teachers

God does not waste time—He uses it with intention, purpose, and precision, even in the seasons that feel slow, confusing, or uncertain. Every season you walk through carries a lesson designed specifically for your growth, whether you recognize it immediately or not. Spring teaches you hope, awakening your faith and reminding you that new beginnings are always possible. Summer teaches you stewardship, challenging you to manage what has been entrusted to you with maturity and discipline. Autumn teaches you release, showing you how to let go of what no longer serves your purpose so you can make room for what's next. Winter teaches you resilience, strengthening your faith and endurance in the face of difficulty and delay. None of these lessons stand alone—they build upon one another. What you learn in one season positions you for revelation in the next, creating a continuous cycle of growth and understanding. Seasons are not random—they are God's curriculum, intentionally designed to shape you into who you are called to become.

Recognizing God's Hand in Every Stage

As you mature spiritually, you begin to notice God in places you once overlooked, recognizing His hand not only in the moments that felt good, but also in the ones that stretched, confused, or even broke you. What once seemed like random or painful experiences begin to take on new meaning. The breakup taught you boundaries, showing you what alignment truly looks like. The delay taught you discipline, strengthening your patience and persistence. The silence taught you trust, deepening your faith when there were no clear answers. The closed door taught you redirection, guiding you away from what was not meant for you and toward what is. When you begin to see your life through this lens, one truth becomes undeniable—nothing was wasted. Every moment, every experience, every season was intentionally woven together by God. Self-discovery is the process of allowing Him to reveal that design, helping you understand that even your detours were part of the direction all along.

Real-World Analogy: The Tapestry of Becoming

Imagine a weaver crafting a tapestry, carefully threading each strand with intention and precision. From the back, it looks chaotic—threads crossing in every direction, colors clashing, patterns unclear, and purpose seemingly absent. It can feel disordered, confusing, and unfinished. But when the fabric is turned around, everything aligns beautifully. What once looked random reveals a deliberate design, a masterpiece woven with care. That is your life. Every thread—whether joyful, painful, or confusing—has been intentionally placed. The moments you understood and the ones you questioned, the seasons that felt clear and the ones that felt chaotic, all become part of the greater picture God is creating. You are not accidental—you are intentional, woven together with purpose, meaning, and divine design.

When You See Yourself Through God's Eyes

Self-discovery isn't perfection — it's progression. It is not the pursuit of flawlessness, but the willingness to keep becoming. Every season of your life peels back another layer of who you truly are, revealing strengths you didn't know you carried, wounds you didn't realize needed healing, and capacities that only pressure could uncover. Growth does not announce itself all at once; it unfolds gradually, layer by layer, season by season. The more honestly you come to know yourself, the more clearly you begin to see God's hand shaping you. What once felt like random experiences start to look intentional. What once felt like delays begin to feel like development. You recognize that even the seasons that confused you were forming you — sharpening your discernment, strengthening your character, and aligning you more closely with who you were created to be. This is the mirror of becoming — not a reflection meant to judge you, but one meant to reveal you. It is sacred because it is honest. It is holy because it is ongoing. And when you learn to honor the process instead of rushing the outcome, you discover that who you are becoming is just as important as where you are going.

Becoming the Person God Envisioned

Self-discovery is holy work, the kind that requires honesty, surrender, and a willingness to see yourself through God's perspective rather than your own limitations. It is the moment you finally begin to recognize the reflection God intended all along—not the version shaped by fear, comparison, or past mistakes, but the one formed by purpose and design. You are not who you were, and you are not yet who you will be, but every step you have taken, every season you have endured, and every revelation you have received has been shaping you into someone capable of carrying purpose with clarity and conviction. Your highs have revealed your gifts, showing you what you are capable of, while your lows have revealed your grit, proving your ability to endure and rise again. Every season has uncovered a different layer of your strength, building a foundation you can now stand on with confidence. And through it all, God has remained both Artist and Advocate—intentionally shaping your life into a living testimony of divine transformation. You now carry the wisdom of every season you have endured, and with that wisdom comes a deeper awareness of who you are becoming. You are not finished—you are becoming. And as this chapter closes, a new one begins. Turn the page—your relationships are about to bloom.

Chapter 7: Relationships in Bloom: Nurturing Connections Through Change

When Growth Requires Community

You cannot thrive in life's seasons without also thriving in your relationships, because growth was never meant to happen in isolation. Transitions test more than your resilience—they test your connections, revealing the strength, depth, and authenticity of the people you are connected to. Every shift, every change, and every moment of personal growth either strengthens your bonds or exposes the cracks that were already present beneath the surface. Relationships are not just additions to your life; they are reflections of it. They act as mirrors that reveal your character, anchors that steady your soul in uncertain times, and fuel that propels you forward into your purpose. Romantic partnerships, friendships, professional networks, and spiritual communities all serve as arenas where empathy is sharpened, trust is cultivated, and your calling becomes clearer. The way you engage in these relationships—how you communicate, support, and grow within them—will ultimately influence not just your journey, but the depth and sustainability of your success.

The Four Pillars of Relational Thriving

To navigate seasons well, relationships must be intentional — not accidental.

- **Romantic (Personal) Relationships**: These connections reveal your heart like nothing else. They require vulnerability, courage, honesty, and a willingness to grow together, not just love together.
- **Platonic (Personal) Relationships**: Friends speak truth when you're drifting, hold you steady when you're discouraged, and celebrate you without competition. They are the chosen family that travels life's seasons with you.
- **Professional Relationships**: Mentorship, collaboration, accountability, and trust shape your opportunities and impact. Your career thrives when your relational skills mature.
- **Spiritual Relationships**: These relationships — mentors, leaders, faith communities — anchor you in God's will and remind you that you're not walking alone.

Section 1: Strengthening Relationships During Transitions

Change Doesn't Break Relationships; It Reveals Them

Transitions expose what relationships are truly made of, revealing their strength, depth, and alignment in ways that comfort never could. As seasons shift, people shift too—priorities evolve, emotions rise to the surface, and expectations begin to stretch in new and sometimes uncomfortable ways. What feels like a gentle breeze to you may feel like a storm to someone else, and that difference in experience can create tension if it is not acknowledged with care and understanding. Romantic partners may grow at different speeds, requiring patience and communication to remain aligned. Friendships may begin to feel the strain of distance, changing responsibilities, or shifting life paths. Professional relationships can become tested under pressure, revealing both strengths and weaknesses in collaboration and trust. Even spiritual connections may be challenged by seasons of doubt, questioning, or transformation. But these relational cracks are not signs of failure—they are invitations. They invite you to communicate more clearly, to love more intentionally, and to strengthen what truly matters rather than ignore what needs attention.

Seeing the Opportunity in Strain

Every relational challenge is an opportunity to grow deeper, not drift apart, if you are willing to approach it with intention, humility, and awareness. These moments of tension are not interruptions—they are invitations to strengthen the foundation of your connections. Romantic relationships teach empathy and sacrifice, requiring you to move beyond yourself and consider the needs and growth of another person. Friendships reveal loyalty and alignment, showing you who is truly walking with you versus who is simply present for convenience. Professional relationships clarify character and collaboration, exposing how you show up under pressure and how well you can work with others toward a common goal. Spiritual relationships reveal whether your connection is rooted in shared values or simply proximity and routine. Change has a way of magnifying authenticity, bringing truth to the surface. Those who stand with you through transitions demonstrate real commitment, while those who drift away often reveal where dependency was mistaken for depth. And even in moments of loss, there is still a lesson—every person who enters your life carries a purpose, even if that purpose is only for a season.

Communication as the Lifeline of Connection

Transitions are communication tests wrapped in discomfort, often revealing how well you express, listen, and respond when things are no longer easy or predictable. In these seasons, what goes unsaid can become just as impactful as what is spoken. Unspoken words begin to form invisible barriers, assumptions quietly create distance, and silence—if left unchecked—breeds confusion that can slowly erode connection. Communication is not optional in these moments; it is essential for survival within any relationship. It requires intentional effort, even when it feels uncomfortable or inconvenient. It may look like reaching out to the friend who feels distant instead of assuming they no longer care, asking your partner how they are truly doing instead of settling for surface-level conversations, clarifying expectations with colleagues to avoid unnecessary tension, or sharing your spiritual struggles with mentors who can guide and support you. When communication is avoided, loneliness begins to grow, even in the presence of others. But when it is embraced with honesty and care, it becomes the bridge that keeps relationships connected, aligned, and strong through every transition.

God as the Guide in Every Connection

Every relationship is ultimately spiritual, whether you recognize it in the moment or not, because God often uses people as instruments in your growth, healing, and direction. He places individuals in your life to heal what has been wounded, to stretch you beyond your comfort, to hold you accountable when you drift, and at times, to redirect you when you are headed in the wrong direction. Relationships are not random—they are purposeful, even when they are challenging. Prayer invites clarity into moments of relational tension, helping you respond with wisdom instead of emotion. Discernment protects you from misalignment, allowing you to recognize who is meant to walk with you and who is not. Grace empowers you to forgive, even when it feels difficult, and wisdom guides you in knowing when to remain committed and when to release what no longer aligns with your growth. When God is invited into the center of your relationships, they begin to function differently—deeper, stronger, and more aligned with purpose..

When Storms Become Soil

Transitions do not destroy strong relationships—they deepen them, revealing a level of connection that comfort alone could never produce. What may feel like tension or discomfort is often an invitation to grow, to become more intentional in how you show up for the people in your life. Every moment of strain presents an opportunity to communicate better, to love deeper, to trust more intentionally, and to reflect God more clearly in your actions and responses. These seasons call you to move beyond surface-level connection and into something more meaningful and mature. And now that you understand how to strengthen relationships in the midst of change, the next step becomes essential—learning how to communicate effectively during these seasons, because connection is only sustained when communication is intentional.

Section 2: Effective Communication in Times of Change

Silence Is as Dangerous as Miscommunication

Words left unsaid often hurt more than words spoken poorly, because silence creates space for assumptions to grow unchecked. In seasons of transition, where emotions are shifting, schedules are changing, and expectations are evolving, what is not communicated can quietly begin to erode even the strongest connections. Partners start to assume instead of ask, friends begin to drift instead of engage, colleagues misinterpret intentions instead of seeking clarity, and spiritual communities miss needs that were never expressed. These small gaps in communication can widen over time, creating distance that feels confusing and unnecessary. That is why clarity is not a luxury in these moments—it is survival. It is the difference between connection and disconnection, between understanding and misunderstanding, between relationships that endure and relationships that slowly fade.

Speaking Truth in Love

Relationships require truth—not harshness, not silence, but truth spoken with love and intention. Real connection cannot thrive where honesty is absent, and growth cannot happen where communication is filtered by fear. It takes courage to speak openly, to tell your partner what genuinely scares you, to express to your friends what you truly need, to communicate clearly with colleagues about what you can realistically manage, and to be vulnerable enough to tell your spiritual leaders when you are struggling. These moments of honesty may feel uncomfortable, but they are necessary for depth and alignment. Truth spoken with love builds bridges, creating understanding and trust that strengthens the relationship. But truth suppressed by fear builds walls, allowing distance, confusion, and resentment to grow over time. The goal is not perfection in communication, but intention—you can be honest without being hurtful, direct without being damaging, and loving without being passive. When truth and love work together, relationships become stronger, clearer, and more resilient.

Listening as a Sacred Skill

Most people listen to respond, not to understand, and that subtle difference has the power to either strengthen or strain every relationship they are part of. During seasons of transition, when emotions are heightened and uncertainty is present, listening becomes holy work. It is no longer just a communication skill—it becomes a ministry. Listening validates what someone is feeling, reassures them that they are not alone, and has the power to bring healing without a single solution being offered. I learned this in a profound way during my time at Alcorn State University through a mentor who left an undeniable imprint on my life, Dr. John Igwebuike, Founder of the Lead Listening Institute. He impressed upon the canvas of my heart that listening is one of the greatest skills never taught, and his teachings and insights on the power of truly hearing people were unmatched. That truth has stayed with me—because real listening is rare, but it is deeply transformative. Sometimes your presence is more powerful than your advice. Sometimes "I hear you" carries more weight than "Here's what to do." In a world that rushes to speak, those who learn to listen create space for trust, connection, and understanding. Listening, at its core, communicates love in its purest and most tangible form.

Divine Guidance in Dialogue

Every meaningful conversation begins with wisdom, not impulse, and not emotion unchecked. The way you approach a conversation often determines the outcome long before a single word is spoken. That is why intentionality matters. Before you speak, pray—invite God into your words so that what you say carries clarity and not confusion. Before you react, pause—create space between what you feel and how you respond so that your emotions do not lead you into regret. Before you assume, ask—because assumptions often distort reality, while questions bring understanding. Scripture reminds us that "a gentle answer turns away wrath," revealing the power of tone, posture, and intention in communication. Grace-filled conversations have the ability to build unity even in the middle of change, tension, or disagreement. They soften what could easily become harsh and bring peace where conflict could have grown. When God is invited into the moment, even the most difficult conversation can become an opportunity for healing, clarity, or reconciliation.

Words Are Seeds

Every word plants something, whether you realize it or not, because your words carry weight, direction, and consequence. Scripture reminds us that the power of life and death lies within the tongue, revealing that what you speak is never neutral—it is either building or breaking, connecting or dividing. God has created us as speaking spirits, meaning that what leaves our mouth has the ability to shape atmospheres, influence relationships, and determine outcomes in ways we often underestimate. When you plant confusion through unclear or careless words, you reap distance. When you plant clarity, you cultivate unity. When you plant empathy, you build trust. When you plant prayer, you create peace. Your words are seeds, and over time, they produce a harvest in your relationships. Communication, then, becomes the watering can—consistently nourishing what you are intentionally planting. But even with the right words, flourishing requires something deeper. It requires the ability to not only support others with presence, truth, and love, but also the humility to receive support when you need it, allowing relationships to function in mutual strength rather than one-sided effort.

Section 3: Supporting Others and Seeking Support

Thriving Alone Is a Myth

No one thrives alone—not even the strongest, most independent soul—because growth was never designed to be sustained in isolation. Transitions have a way of intensifying every area of life. Responsibilities begin to shift, emotions deepen in ways you didn't expect, and workloads increase, often all at once. What once felt manageable can quickly become overwhelming if you try to carry it by yourself. In these moments, relationships are tested not just by how clearly you communicate or how close you feel, but by your ability to both give and receive support well. It requires humility to admit when you need help and maturity to show up consistently for others when they do. Strength is not found in doing everything alone—it is revealed in knowing when to lean and when to lift. Because trying to navigate change without help isn't strength—it is slow destruction, draining your energy, distorting your perspective, and isolating you from the very connections that were meant to sustain you.

The Power of Being Present

Support begins with presence—not perfection, not quick fixes, and not performance, but simply being there in a way that is genuine and consistent. In a world that often rushes to solve, advise, or impress, presence stands apart because it chooses connection over correction. It does not require you to have all the answers; it only asks that you be available, attentive, and sincere. Presence communicates what words sometimes cannot: "I see you," "I'm here," and "You're not alone." These simple yet powerful truths create a sense of safety and reassurance in moments when life feels overwhelming. Whether it is a partner navigating stress, a friend walking through grief, a colleague facing uncertainty, or a spiritual companion wrestling with doubt, your willingness to show up becomes more than support—it becomes ministry. In those moments, your presence carries weight, offering comfort, stability, and a reminder that no one has to walk through their season alone.

Receiving Help as Strength, Not Weakness

Asking for help often feels vulnerable, and accepting help can feel even more uncomfortable, especially when you are used to carrying things on your own. For many, strength has been defined by independence, by the ability to manage, solve, and endure without needing others. I know this personally, because even as I write this, it is an area I am still learning in—allowing God to open me up, to soften the parts of me that resist receiving, and to trust that I was never meant to carry everything alone. But the truth remains: vulnerability is where intimacy grows, and receiving is where pride begins to die. God often chooses to send provision through people—through their presence, their wisdom, their support, and their prayers. And when you refuse help, you may unknowingly refuse the very blessing He is trying to release into your life. There is strength in allowing others to carry what feels heavy, in letting mentors guide your career, in allowing friends to support your heart, and in trusting spiritual leaders to cover you in prayer. Interdependence is not weakness—it is biblical. It reflects the design of community, where we are meant to support one another, grow together, and walk through every season not in isolation, but in connection.

Reciprocity and Relational Flourishing

Healthy support is not one-sided—it is reciprocal, built on a rhythm of mutual care, contribution, and connection. In strong relationships, there is a natural exchange where you pour and they pour, where you learn and they grow, where you uplift and they steady you in return. This balance is not always perfectly even in every moment, but over time, it creates a foundation of trust that allows the relationship to endure seasons of pressure, stress, and change. When support flows in only one direction for too long, it can lead to exhaustion on one side and dependency on the other. That is why awareness matters. You should never feel like the only giver, constantly pouring without being replenished, nor should you remain in a position where you are only receiving without learning how to contribute. True support is strongest when it moves in both directions, creating a partnership where both individuals are strengthened, valued, and sustained through every season they walk through together.

The Rope That Holds You Through Storms

Your relational network is like a rope woven from many strands, each one representing a different connection, a different person, a different source of strength in your life. On their own, each strand has limitations—only able to carry so much weight before it begins to strain. But when those strands are woven together, something powerful is formed—something resilient, something unbreakable. That is what healthy relationships create when they are nurtured with intention. Support, both given and received, is what weaves that rope, strengthening each connection and reinforcing the whole. It is built through presence, honesty, trust, and mutual care over time. And because of it, you are able to withstand storms that you would never survive alone. What would have overwhelmed you in isolation becomes manageable in community, reminding you that you were never meant to carry life's weight by yourself.

Blossoms in Every Season

Relationships bloom when they are intentionally nurtured, not neglected or left to chance. Through this journey, you have learned how to strengthen connections in the midst of uncertainty, how to communicate clearly when emotions shift, and how to both give and receive support in a way that builds rather than drains. When these elements come together, relationships move beyond simply surviving seasons of change—they become sanctuaries, spaces where growth is cultivated, resilience is reinforced, and connection is deepened. Every conversation you engage in, every moment of support you offer or receive, and every act of presence you extend becomes a seed planted into the soil of your relational life, eventually growing into fruit that can sustain you for years to come. As you move into the next season, carry this truth with you: strong roots produce beautiful blooms. You have tended your relational garden with intention, and now it is time to shift your focus toward the next major season of your life. Ahead lies a crossroads where purpose, calling, opportunity, transition, fear, ambition, and identity all collide, demanding clarity and courage. This is not just about what you will do—it is about who you will become. Turn the page. It is time to step into your professional purpose.

Chapter 8: Career Crossroads: Finding Purpose in Professional Transitions

Your Career Is More Than a Paycheck

Your career isn't just a paycheck — it's a reflection of your purpose, your values, and the season you're in. Most people stumble through professional transitions unprepared, chasing stability instead of calling and comfort instead of growth. But your career crossroads aren't random interruptions — they are divine intersections where opportunity, preparation, and revelation meet. How you navigate these seasons shapes far more than your bank account. It molds your confidence. It refines your character. It strengthens your calling. Every promotion you don't get, every job you leave, every interview you fail, every door that closes is a signpost pointing toward your purpose — *if you're willing to read it.*

The Seasons of Professional Life

Just as the natural world moves through seasons, your career unfolds in cycles God intentionally orchestrates.

- **Spring (Planting Skills and Knowledge)**: The early stages of your career are about learning, experimenting, and discovering strengths. The seeds you sow now — discipline, curiosity, humility — become the foundation for future opportunities.
- **Summer (Growth and Expansion)**: This is the season where responsibility grows, visibility increases, and opportunities expand. But fruit comes only if you remain adaptable, teachable, and strategically positioned.
- **Autumn (Reflection and Adjustment)**: Mid-career moments often require assessment. Are you aligned with your gifts or drifting into obligation? This is a season of refinement, not regret.
- **Winter (Resilience and Repositioning)**: Job loss. Burnout. Reorganization. Missed promotions. Winter feels harsh, but it is the season where God strengthens your roots and prepares you for a new assignment.

Section 1: Navigating Career Changes and Transitions

Discomfort Is Often Your First Calling

Career transitions rarely arrive at convenient times. They tend to show up when you feel exhausted, unsure of your next step, or deeply craving stability and clarity. Instead of aligning with your sense of readiness, they disrupt your comfort, shake your confidence, and push you toward unfamiliar paths that require more faith than certainty. In these moments, it can feel like everything is being unsettled at once—your plans, your identity, and even your sense of direction. But the discomfort you feel is not a warning to retreat; it is a signal to pay attention. It is often the indicator that something within you has outgrown its current environment. God frequently uses tension as an announcement that a season is coming to an end, creating just enough uneasiness to move you out of what is familiar and into what is next.

Recognizing When Change Is Needed

Professional seasons do not always shift in obvious or dramatic ways; sometimes the transition is subtle, unfolding quietly through a slow but persistent sense of dissatisfaction that you cannot ignore. Other times, it arrives abruptly through circumstances like a layoff, a leadership change, or an unexpected disruption that forces movement whether you feel ready or not. In some seasons, the shift is emotional, revealed through burnout, exhaustion, or a deep spiritual misalignment that makes what once felt meaningful now feel heavy. In others, it becomes logical, evident through capped growth, limited opportunity, or the realization that where you are can no longer take you where you are meant to go. The signs, when you pause to acknowledge them, are often clear—you begin to feel unchallenged or undervalued, your work starts to drain you both spiritually and emotionally, you struggle to envision a future in your current environment, and your personal values no longer align with the culture around you. These moments are not indicators of failure; they are divine nudges, invitations to reassess, realign, and move forward. Ignoring them keeps you stagnant, but honoring them positions you to step into greater purpose with clarity and intention.

The Role of Faith in Transition

Uncertainty is not a problem for God—it is often His preferred classroom, the place where He teaches you to trust Him beyond what you can see or control. What feels unclear to you is never confusing to Him. In these moments, He invites you closer, not to give you all the answers at once, but to shape your dependence on Him. Prayer begins to reveal clarity, not always by changing your situation immediately, but by aligning your heart and perspective with His will. Scripture provides grounding, anchoring you in truth when your emotions feel unstable. Discernment begins to redirect your path, helping you recognize what is for you and what is not, even when the difference is subtle. And spiritual counsel reinforces wisdom, placing voices in your life that can see what you may not yet understand. When you look at Joseph's journey, it did not resemble progress—he walked through slavery, endured setbacks, and faced imprisonment. Yet every disruption was preparation, every delay was development, and every closed door was positioning him for what God had already ordained. Your career transitions often work the same way. What feels like loss may actually be alignment, and what looks like a setback is often a divine setup for something greater than you could have planned on your own.

Practical Steps to Navigate Change

1. **Assess Your Current Landscape**: Take an honest and intentional inventory of where you are right now—what is working well, what is no longer serving you, what truly matters at this stage of your life, and what must change in order for you to grow. This requires clarity, not comfort, and the willingness to confront both your satisfaction and your dissatisfaction without filtering the truth.
2. **Clarify Your Calling**: Go beyond surface-level thinking and begin to explore what is truly being stirred within you.
    a. What strengths consistently light you up and make you feel alive, energized, and aligned with your purpose?
    b. What burdens or frustrations weigh you down and signal areas that may no longer be meant for you?
    c. What dreams, ideas, or visions continue to resurface, even when you try to ignore them? These patterns are often clues pointing toward your deeper calling.
3. **Take Calculated Risks**: Transitions are not fulfilled through intention alone—they require movement. This may look like learning new skills, applying for new opportunities, building new connections, or stepping outside of your comfort zone in ways

that stretch your capacity. The goal is not reckless action, but faith-filled strategy—moving forward with wisdom while trusting God in the unknown.

4. **Build Your Support Network**: You were never meant to navigate career transitions alone. Surround yourself with mentors who can guide you, advisors who can challenge your thinking, and advocates who can open doors you cannot access on your own. Growth accelerates in the presence of the right people, and career change becomes more sustainable when it is supported by a strong, intentional network.

The Fork in the Road

Transitions are not threats to your stability—they are invitations to your destiny, calling you beyond what is comfortable into what is purposeful. The safe path will always feel familiar, predictable, and secure, but it rarely stretches you into the fullness of who you are meant to become. In contrast, the steep path—the one that feels uncertain, challenging, and even intimidating—is often the very place where transformation takes place. It demands growth, courage, and faith, requiring you to move forward even when you cannot see every step ahead. Purpose rarely resides on the easy path, because it is forged in the spaces that require more from you than you initially believe you have. It is shaped through pressure, refined through uncertainty, and revealed through obedience. Now that you understand when and why career transitions occur, the next step becomes essential—uncovering the passions within you that point toward your true calling and guide you into the life you were created to live.

Section 2: Identifying Passions and Aligning with Purpose

You Can't Flourish in Someone Else's Dream

Many people choose careers based on expectations, pressure, or fear—following paths that seem practical, approved, or safe rather than aligned with who they truly are. They pursue what is expected of them, what others have modeled, or what feels secure in the moment, often ignoring the deeper pull within their spirit. But God did not design you to simply perform tasks or fulfill roles—He designed you to make an impact, to bring something unique into the world that only you can carry. Passion, therefore, is not optional; it is a compass, guiding you toward the spaces where your gifts, energy, and purpose intersect. It points you toward what matters, what moves you, and what aligns with your design. And purpose is not random or accidental—it is revealed over time, through obedience, awareness, and a willingness to follow where God is leading.

The Divine Design of Passion

God often hides purpose in the very things that stir something deep within you—the things that energize you when you engage with them, move you emotionally in ways you cannot ignore, challenge you to grow beyond your current capacity, burden your heart with a desire to see change, and inspire you to imagine something greater than what currently exists. These moments are not random or insignificant; they are intentional signals pointing toward what you were created to carry. What captures your attention consistently is often connected to what God has placed within you uniquely. These passions are not coincidences—they are divine fingerprints, marks of purpose woven into your identity. However, passion alone is not enough to sustain impact. When passion is aligned with your gifting, refined through your calling, and positioned within the right opportunities, it becomes something powerful—something focused, effective, and ultimately unstoppable in the hands of God.

When Passion Feels Hidden or Conflicted

Some seasons have a way of burying your passions beneath the weight of survival, routine, or fear, making it feel like the things that once excited you have faded or disappeared altogether. Responsibilities increase, life becomes demanding, and what once felt alive within you can become quiet and distant. But this does not mean those passions are gone—it simply means they are waiting—waiting for the right environment, the right alignment, and the right level of obedience to bring them back to the surface. Even Moses spent years in obscurity, tending sheep in the wilderness after once being positioned in a place of influence. It could have looked like his purpose was lost, buried under failure and distance from what he once knew. But when he encountered God and aligned himself with the call placed on his life, everything shifted—his voice, his leadership, and his purpose were awakened for a mission far greater than he had imagined. The same principle applies to you. Your hidden passions are not waiting for applause, validation, or perfect conditions—they are waiting for alignment. When what is within you aligns with what God is calling you to do, what once felt buried will begin to rise with clarity, confidence, and purpose.

Practical Steps to Identify Your Passion

1. **Reflect on Joyful Engagement**: Take intentional time to identify the activities, environments, and moments where you feel most alive, energized, and fully present. Pay attention to what captures your attention without force—what you naturally lean into, what excites your spirit, and what gives you a sense of fulfillment even when it requires effort.
2. **Assess Your Skills and Strengths**: Evaluate where your natural abilities and developed skills intersect with what you genuinely enjoy. Consider the areas where you consistently perform with excellence, where others recognize your value, and where your competence aligns with your passion—because purpose often lives at the intersection of what you're good at and what you love.
3. **Seek God's Guidance**: Invite God into your process with intentionality, not just asking for direction, but seeking alignment. Through prayer, reflection, and time in His presence, allow Him to bring clarity to your ambitions, refine your desires, and redirect anything that is rooted in pressure rather than purpose.
4. **Experiment and Explore**: Do not wait for perfect clarity before taking action. Step out, try new things, test ideas, and allow experience to reveal what theory cannot. Movement creates understanding. Purpose is not only discovered through thinking—it is uncovered through doing, refining, and adjusting as you grow.

The Lighthouse and the Ship

Your passion is a lighthouse, steady and intentional, designed to guide you even when everything around you feels uncertain. The waves may be rough, crashing against your confidence and testing your resolve. The night may be dark, making it difficult to see clearly or understand where you are headed. There will be moments when doubt rises and direction feels distant. But the light remains. If you choose to follow it—consistently, faithfully, and with trust—it will keep you aligned with your purpose. It may not reveal the entire journey at once, but it will always give you enough direction to keep moving forward without drifting away from what you were created to do.

Section 3: Strategies for Professional Fulfillment

Success Without Fulfillment Is Failure in Disguise

You can climb ladders and still feel empty, reaching new levels of success that look impressive on the outside but leave you unfulfilled on the inside. You can earn more money and still feel purposeless, realizing that financial gain alone cannot satisfy the deeper longing within your spirit. You can impress others with your achievements, your titles, and your progress, yet still carry a quiet disappointment within yourself because you know you are not fully aligned with who you were created to be. These realities reveal a deeper truth—fulfillment is not accidental; it is cultivated. It is built intentionally through alignment with purpose, through choices that honor your calling, and through a life that reflects not just external success, but internal clarity and meaning.

The Pillars of Fulfillment

1. **Clarity of Vision**: Develop a deep understanding of why you do the work you do, not just the tasks you perform each day. When your "why" is clear, your work gains meaning, direction, and purpose beyond titles or responsibilities. Vision anchors you in seasons of difficulty and keeps you aligned when distractions arise.
2. **Continuous Growth**: Commit to lifelong learning and development, both personally and professionally. Growth is not optional if you desire to lead effectively and evolve with purpose. The moment you stop learning, you begin to plateau, and what once worked will no longer sustain where you are going.
3. **Balance and Boundaries**: Establish healthy rhythms that protect your time, energy, and well-being. Rest is not a luxury—it is spiritual, necessary for clarity, sustainability, and long-term effectiveness. Without boundaries, even meaningful work can become overwhelming and misaligned.
4. **Serving Others**: Anchor your work in impact, not just achievement. Fulfillment is not found in what you accumulate, but in how you contribute. When your work serves others and creates value beyond yourself, it produces a deeper sense of purpose that success alone cannot provide.

When Challenges Arise

Every career will face moments that test its foundation—industry shifts that disrupt what once felt stable, leadership changes that alter direction and expectations, seasons of burnout that drain your energy, rejection that challenges your confidence, and delays that stretch your patience. These are not isolated obstacles; they are inevitable parts of the journey, and they serve a deeper purpose. They test your commitment to what you are called to do, revealing whether your motivation is rooted in purpose or in external validation. In moments like these, it becomes easy to chase what is trending, to seek approval, or to adjust your path based on what seems most rewarding in the moment. But staying aligned requires discipline and conviction. Even Paul the Apostle faced constant opposition—imprisonment, rejection, persecution, and delay—yet he never abandoned his calling. His mission was not driven by comfort or applause, but by obedience and purpose. Because of that alignment, his impact extended far beyond his circumstances and continues to influence generations. The same is true for you. When you remain aligned with what God has placed on your life, your impact will not be temporary—it will be lasting.

Practical Strategies for Fulfilled Work

1. **Create a Purpose Statement**: Take the time to clearly define your "why"—the deeper reason behind your work, your ambition, and your direction. This becomes your North Star, guiding your decisions, anchoring you in uncertain seasons, and keeping you aligned when distractions or opportunities try to pull you off course.
2. **Set Intentional Goals**: Break your larger vision into small, actionable steps that you can consistently pursue. Progress is built through discipline and consistency, not just inspiration. Each small step creates momentum, and over time, that momentum compounds into meaningful, measurable growth.
3. **Seek Mentorship and Community**: Surround yourself with individuals who can provide wisdom, accountability, and perspective. Mentors help you avoid unnecessary mistakes, while community offers encouragement and support. Growth accelerates when you are not navigating your journey alone.
4. **Regular Reflection**: Build a rhythm of reviewing where you are, refining what needs adjustment, and realigning with your purpose. Reflection allows you to stay intentional, correct course when needed, and ensure that your actions continue to match your calling. Fulfillment is not a one-time achievement—it is a lifestyle cultivated through consistent awareness and alignment.

The Gardener and the Orchard

A garden does not bear fruit simply because a seed was planted once; it thrives because it is cultivated consistently over time. It requires attention, patience, and intentional care—watering, pruning, protecting, and nurturing what has been planted so it can grow to its full potential. Without that ongoing investment, even the best seeds can fail to produce what they were designed to become. Your career is no different. It is not sustained by a single decision, a one-time opportunity, or a moment of inspiration, but by consistent effort, continuous growth, and intentional alignment with your purpose. What you nurture will grow, and what you neglect will wither, making cultivation the difference between potential and fulfillment.

The Season of Purposeful Work

Your career crossroads are not detours—they are direction, guiding you toward alignment with what you were created to do rather than pulling you away from it. What once felt like uncertainty now begins to reveal itself as intentional movement, shaping your path with purpose. You have learned how to navigate transition with awareness, identify the passions that point toward your calling, and align your work with what God has placed within you. Like a tree rooted deeply in the ground yet reaching boldly toward the sun, your career has the potential to be both stable and expansive—grounded in purpose while continuously growing into new levels of impact. The work you commit to today is not isolated; it is building the foundation for the influence you will carry tomorrow. You have learned how to thrive professionally, how to move with intention and clarity in your career. But your life is not meant to be one-dimensional. Now, it is time to expand your focus and explore how to nurture every other part of your life—your body, your mind, your spirit, and your emotional well-being. Because while thriving in your career is powerful, thriving in your whole life is transformational. Turn the page. Health and harmony await.

Chapter 9: Health and Harmony: Wellness Strategies for Every Season

The Foundation Beneath Every Season

You cannot truly thrive in life if you neglect your body, your mind, or your spirit, because health is not optional—it is foundational to everything you are called to carry. It is easy to overlook in the moment, to push past exhaustion, ignore imbalance, or delay care for the sake of productivity or progress. But neglect does not disappear—it accumulates. It may not show consequences today, but seasons of neglect will always demand payment later. Every choice you make about how you treat yourself—what you eat, how you move, how you think, how you rest—becomes either a deposit into or a withdrawal from your future vitality. The life you experience tomorrow is being shaped by the decisions you make today. Your clarity five years from now is directly connected to how you train your mind in the present. Your strength in the next season is influenced by how you care for your body now. Your peace in moments of transition is sustained by how consistently you nurture your spirit today. What you invest in your well-being in this season will determine not only how you endure what is ahead, but how stable, aligned, and effective you will be in every season to come.

The True Cost of Ignoring Wellness

Life's transitions require resilience, yet many find themselves overwhelmed and depleted because their well-being has gone unattended for far too long. What should be seasons of growth become seasons of struggle when the foundation is weak. Physical fatigue begins to slow your progress, making even simple tasks feel heavy. Mental stress clouds your judgment, causing you to question decisions you would normally make with clarity. Emotional depletion erodes your confidence, leaving you uncertain and discouraged. Spiritual dryness weakens your discernment, making it harder to recognize God's direction in critical moments. This is why your well-being cannot be treated as secondary. God created your body as a temple to be cared for and honored, and your mind as a garden to be cultivated with intention. If either is neglected, your ability to walk fully in your purpose becomes compromised. Seasons of transition have a way of magnifying what you have ignored, bringing hidden weaknesses to the surface. But when you choose intentional wellness—caring for your body, renewing your mind, and nurturing your spirit—you position yourself to move through those same seasons with strength, clarity, and endurance. What once felt overwhelming becomes manageable, and what once threatened to break you becomes the very thing that proves you are unshakable.

Why Wellness Must Be Holistic

Wellness is not simply a gym routine, a diet plan, or an occasional self-care day—it is far deeper than any temporary practice or surface-level habit. True wellness is integration, the intentional harmony between your physical health, your mental clarity, your emotional resilience, and your spiritual alignment. These dimensions are not separate—they are interconnected, each one influencing and reinforcing the others. When your body is strengthened, your mind becomes sharper and more focused. When your spirit is nourished, your energy expands and your perspective deepens. When your emotions are balanced, your decisions become clearer and more grounded. Wellness, then, is not about isolated efforts—it is about cultivating a lifestyle where every part of you is being developed with intention. This chapter is designed to guide you toward habits that elevate every dimension of your life, not in a way that is temporary or unsustainable, but in a way that produces lasting strength, stability, and alignment across every season you walk through.

Section 1: Prioritizing Physical and Mental Well-Being

Neglect Is a Silent Thief

Your body and mind never forget how you treat them, even when you try to overlook the impact in the moment. Every skipped meal, every all-nighter, every unprocessed thought, and every stress-filled week leaves an imprint, slowly shaping your capacity, your energy, and your resilience over time. These choices may seem small or insignificant in isolation, but when repeated, they begin to accumulate, quietly eroding your strength and stability from within. What you dismiss today eventually demands attention tomorrow. Life's transitions are already challenging, requiring clarity, endurance, and focus—but when you add the weight of your own neglect, those challenges become heavier than they were ever meant to be. What could have been navigated with strength begins to feel overwhelming, not because the season is impossible, but because your foundation has been weakened. How you care for yourself now determines how well you will carry what comes next.

The Interconnectedness of Body and Mind

Your physical and mental health are in constant conversation, continuously influencing one another in ways that cannot be separated or ignored. What affects one will inevitably impact the other. Stress, for example, does not remain confined to your thoughts—it begins to affect your body, disrupting digestion and weakening your overall physical state. Poor sleep does more than leave you tired; it damages your focus, clouds your thinking, and limits your ability to make sound decisions. Anxiety does not stay hidden in the mind—it manifests physically, showing up in tension, fatigue, and imbalance. At the same time, physical strength and care support mental stability, providing the energy and resilience needed to think clearly and respond effectively. These systems are interconnected by design, meaning you cannot neglect one without compromising the other. True thriving requires an intentional commitment to both, recognizing that your well-being is not divided—it is integrated.

Practical Steps to Prioritize Yourself

1. Physical Check-Ins
    a. Pause regularly and take an honest inventory of how your body is truly feeling, rather than pushing through without awareness.
    b. Evaluate your energy levels—are you consistently energized, or are you running on empty and relying on temporary fixes?
    c. Assess your movement—are you incorporating intentional activity that strengthens and supports your body, or remaining stagnant for long periods?
    d. Reflect on your nutrition—are you fueling your body with what it needs to sustain strength, clarity, and endurance?
    e. Remember that simple, consistent adjustments—when maintained over time—create long-term gains that strengthen your foundation for every season.
2. Mental Space
    a. Guard your thoughts with intention by limiting exposure to negativity, reducing unnecessary social media noise, and clearing emotional clutter that overwhelms your focus.

    b. Create space for practices that recalibrate your mind, such as journaling to process your thoughts, prayer to align your spirit, and meditation to restore clarity and calm.
3. Routine as Armor
    a. Establish routines that protect your stability and create structure in your daily life, especially during seasons of transition and uncertainty.
    b. Prioritize sleep, balanced meals, and intentional movement—not as optional habits, but as essential disciplines that sustain your strength, sharpen your focus, and support your overall well-being.

Real-World Analogy: The Athlete Preparing for the Big Game

An athlete does not train only on the field; their performance is shaped long before the game ever begins. They sleep strategically, understanding that rest is essential for recovery and endurance. They eat intentionally, fueling their body with what it needs to perform at a high level. They rest faithfully, recognizing that overexertion without restoration leads to burnout. They prepare mentally, strengthening their focus, discipline, and ability to respond under pressure. Every detail matters, because every detail contributes to the outcome. Life's transitions function in the same way—they are your championship season, the moments that require your best, your sharpest, and your most prepared self. But without intentional preparation, you will not step into these seasons equipped—you will arrive exhausted, overwhelmed, and underprepared for what is required.

The Sacred Act of Prioritizing Yourself

Prioritizing yourself is not selfish—it is sacred, because you cannot pour into others from a place of depletion and expect to sustain impact. The investment you make in your body and mind today does not just affect the present moment; it pays dividends in your future clarity, endurance, and peace. Every intentional choice—resting when needed, setting boundaries, nurturing your thoughts, and caring for your physical well-being—builds a stronger, more stable version of you. And when you show up for yourself in these ways, you naturally show up better for God, for your relationships, and for your purpose. You become more present, more grounded, and more aligned with what you are called to carry. Now that your foundation is set, it is time to go deeper—into holistic wellness, the integrated approach that allows every part of your life to flourish together rather than function in isolation.

Section 2: Holistic Approaches to Health During Life's Changes

One-Wall Health Cannot Hold Your Life

Most people tend to focus on one area of their health while neglecting the others, believing that progress in a single dimension is enough to sustain them. But caring only for your body while ignoring your mind, or strengthening your mind while neglecting your spirit, creates an imbalance that cannot hold under pressure. It is like building a house with only one wall—no matter how strong that wall may be, collapse is inevitable because the structure lacks full support. Life's transitions have a way of revealing these gaps, exposing what has been overlooked or underdeveloped. In moments of pressure, what you have neglected will surface, and if one part of you is weak, the rest of you will begin to feel unstable. True strength is not found in isolated growth, but in intentional development across every part of your life.

The Four Pillars of Holistic Health

1. **Physical Health — Stewarding the Temple** – Fuel your body. Move consistently. Rest intentionally. Your body carries your purpose — treat it like it matters.
2. **Mental Health — Training the Mind** – Your thoughts shape your direction. Mindfulness, boundaries, and reflection guard your peace.
3. **Emotional Health — Honoring What You Feel** – Emotions are messengers. Listen to them, but don't let them run your life. Healthy processing prevents unhealthy reactions.
4. **Spiritual Health — Aligning with God's Perspective** – Your spirit is your compass. Prayer, worship, reflection, and scripture anchor your identity and guide your choices. When these four elements move together, you create harmony that sustains you through any season.

When Seasons Disrupt Balance

New jobs, new relationships, seasons of grief, moments of uncertainty, and the weight of ongoing stress all have the ability to disrupt your rhythm and scatter your focus in ways that feel overwhelming. Transitions rarely come with simplicity; they often arrive layered, demanding your attention in multiple areas at once. What once felt steady can quickly become fragmented, pulling your energy in different directions and leaving you feeling uncentered. But this is where holistic practices become essential. They do more than support you—they anchor you. They create stability within you even when everything around you is shifting. Instead of being pulled by every change, you become grounded, able to move with clarity, intention, and balance. Holistic practices keep you centered, reminding you that even in the midst of transition, you can remain rooted and steady.

Real-World Analogy — The Orchestra of Life

Your life is a symphony, a complex and intentional composition where every part plays a critical role in the overall sound you produce. Your physical health acts as the percussion, setting the rhythm and providing the foundational energy that drives you forward. Your mental health is like the strings, shaping clarity, focus, and the tone of your thoughts. Your emotional health functions as the woodwinds, expressing depth, sensitivity, and the way you process and respond to what you feel. And your spiritual health stands as the brass, bold and anchoring, carrying your identity, your purpose, and your connection to God. Each section is distinct, yet deeply interconnected. When one area falls out of tune, the entire composition begins to suffer, creating imbalance and dissonance in your life. But holistic health steps in as the conductor, intentionally bringing each part into alignment—restoring balance, establishing rhythm, and creating harmony so that your life produces a sound that is not only stable, but powerful and whole.

Integration Creates Stability

Holistic wellness is not optional—it is essential, serving as the operating system for a fulfilled, peaceful, and resilient life. It is what allows every part of you to function in alignment, rather than in conflict, creating a foundation that can sustain you through both calm and challenging seasons. When your physical, mental, emotional, and spiritual health are working together, you are no longer easily shaken by change. Transitions that once felt overwhelming begin to feel purposeful, no longer derailing your progress but refining your character and strengthening your capacity. Instead of reacting to life, you begin to move through it with intention, clarity, and stability. But understanding holistic wellness is only the beginning. The next step is learning how to build consistent habits that reinforce this way of living—habits that keep you grounded, disciplined, and aligned, even in the hardest seasons.

Section 3: Establishing Habits for Sustained Well-Being

Motivation Won't Save You; Habits Will

Motivation is fleeting, rising and falling depending on how you feel in the moment. Inspiration, while powerful, is temporary, often sparked by a moment but difficult to sustain over time. Even excitement, though energizing at first, eventually fades when faced with routine, pressure, or fatigue. But habits outlast emotion. They remain when feelings change, when circumstances shift, and when life becomes demanding. This is why transitions become such powerful tests—they expose your routines, revealing which habits were built with intention and discipline and which were built on convenience and inconsistency. What once felt easy may no longer hold under pressure if it was not rooted in structure. If you truly desire wellness that lasts, you must move beyond relying on how you feel and begin creating systems that support you regardless of your emotional state—systems that remain steady, even when life is not.

The Power of Small, Consistent Actions

It is not always the big, life-altering decisions that shape your future—it is the tiny, consistent choices you make every single day. The seemingly small actions, often overlooked or dismissed, are the ones that quietly build the foundation of your life over time. Choosing to drink water instead of neglecting your hydration, taking a walk to move your body, resting intentionally rather than pushing through exhaustion, praying consistently to stay spiritually aligned, and journaling for even five minutes to process your thoughts—these are not insignificant habits. They are building blocks. Each small action, repeated with consistency, begins to stack upon the other, creating momentum that eventually transforms into a lifestyle. What feels minor in the moment becomes major over time, shaping not only your habits, but your health, your mindset, and your overall well-being

Creating a Sustainable Framework

1. **Anchor Your Day**: Establish intentional habits at the beginning and end of your day that ground you, center your thoughts, and

align your focus. How you start your morning sets the tone for everything that follows, and how you end your night determines how well you reset for what's next. These anchor points create stability, especially in seasons of transition.

2. **Prioritize Progress Over Perfection**: Focus on consistent, forward movement rather than waiting for flawless execution. Perfection often leads to paralysis, while progress builds momentum. Small, imperfect actions done consistently will always outperform occasional bursts of intensity that cannot be sustained.
3. **Stack Your Habits**: Integrate new habits into routines you already have by attaching them to existing behaviors. This creates natural rhythms that are easier to maintain. For example, pairing prayer with your morning routine or journaling before bed helps reinforce consistency without overwhelming your schedule.
4. **Track and Reflect**: Pay attention to your habits, your patterns, and your progress over time. Tracking creates awareness, and awareness breeds accountability. When you regularly reflect on what is working and what needs adjustment, you position yourself to grow intentionally rather than operate on autopilot.

Overcoming the Season's Obstacles

Transitions disrupt routines—and that is completely normal. Life does not always move in predictable patterns, and seasons of change will often interrupt even the most well-established habits. But disruption does not have to lead to abandonment. The key is to build flexibility into your habits so they can adapt with your life rather than collapse under pressure. Rigid routines may work in stable seasons, but sustainable habits are the ones that can bend without breaking when life shifts. The goal is not perfection, nor is it flawless consistency every single day. The goal is return—returning to what grounds you, what strengthens you, and what keeps you aligned, even after interruption. It is the ability to reset without guilt, to realign without shame, and to continue forward with intention, knowing that consistency is not about never falling off, but about always coming back sustains you.

Real-World Analogy – The Gardener's Routine

A garden does not grow simply because you watered it once; it flourishes because you tend to it consistently, giving it the attention, care, and nourishment it needs over time. Growth is not the result of a single moment of effort, but of repeated, intentional investment. At the same time, weeds do not wait for your motivation to appear—they grow regardless, creeping in when left unattended. In the same way, growth does not wait for your mood; it requires discipline beyond how you feel in the moment. Wellness operates by the same principle. It is not built on occasional effort or bursts of inspiration, but through cultivation—steady, intentional, and loving care that is practiced daily. What you consistently nurture will thrive, and what you neglect will eventually decline.

Mastery Through Repetition

Well-being is not built in a single moment of effort or a one-time decision to do better—it is built through momentum, through the consistent choices you make day after day. It is the accumulation of small, intentional actions that gradually shape your strength, your clarity, and your stability over time. What you do repeatedly becomes what you rely on. The systems you create today—your habits, your routines, your disciplines—become the very foundation you stand on tomorrow. In moments when life feels demanding or uncertain, you will not rise to the level of your intentions; you will fall to the level of your systems. And if those systems are built with care, consistency, and purpose, they will carry you with strength into whatever season comes next.

The Symphony of Balance

Your body, mind, emotions, and spirit are instruments in a lifelong symphony, each one designed to play a vital role in the overall sound of your life. Every season you walk through challenges you to engage these instruments with greater intentionality, deeper discipline, and a stronger sense of harmony. When one area is neglected, the music becomes disjointed, but when all parts are aligned, your life begins to produce something powerful and whole. When you embrace holistic wellness—supported by consistent habits and anchored in spiritual alignment—you move beyond simply surviving transitions and begin to flourish through them with clarity and strength. Health, then, is not a destination you arrive at once and maintain effortlessly; it is a lifestyle that must be cultivated daily. It is worship, honoring God through how you care for what He has entrusted to you. It is stewardship, recognizing that your well-being is a responsibility, not an afterthought. It is alignment with God's design for your life, allowing every part of you to function as it was created to. Every choice you make becomes a note, every habit you build becomes a chord, and every season you endure becomes a movement within the greater composition. Together, they form the soundtrack of your thriving life.

And now that your wellness foundation is secure, you are ready to explore the final dimension of thriving in transition—your legacy.

Chapter 10: Legacy and Longevity: Crafting a Meaningful Life Journey

The Season That Outlives You

Life does not simply happen—it is authored, shaped moment by moment through the decisions you make and the paths you choose to follow. And whether you realize it or not, you are writing your story in real time, crafting a narrative that is unfolding with every passing day. Every choice becomes a sentence, adding meaning and direction to your journey. Every season becomes a chapter, marking growth, challenge, and transformation. Every act of courage, every moment of kindness, and every step of obedience contributes to the plotline of your life, forming a story that is uniquely yours. You will leave a story behind—one that others will read through your impact, your influence, and your example. The question is not if you will leave a legacy, but whether that story will reflect purpose, intention, and the divine design God placed within you. Legacy is not something that begins at the end of your life; it is the thread woven through every chapter you have already lived, shaping the meaning of your story long before it is complete lived.

Section 1: Creating a Meaningful Life Narrative

Your Life Is a Story You Are Responsible For

Many people drift through life unaware that their daily decisions are shaping a narrative that future generations will one day inherit, leaving behind patterns, principles, and examples that extend far beyond their own lifetime. But meaningful lives do not happen by accident—they are formed through intentional authorship, through deliberate choices that are aligned with both calling and character. You are not just a passive participant in your story; you are an active contributor, both the character living it and the one making decisions that shape its direction. Yet even in that responsibility, there is a greater truth—God, in His sovereignty, remains the ultimate Author. He is not distant from your story; He is deeply involved, intentional, and aware of every detail. In His wisdom, He has chosen to consider you, to involve you, and to entrust you with real decisions that carry real weight. He places the pen in your hands, not to surrender His authority, but to invite your obedience. Your choices matter, your actions carry meaning, and your life reflects the partnership between divine purpose and human response. When you align your decisions with His design, your story begins to reflect not just your intentions, but His greater narrative unfolding through you.

Understanding the Author Within

A meaningful narrative does not emerge by chance—it is shaped through intentional living, through choices that are made with awareness rather than passivity. It requires you to live with purpose, not drifting through life reacting to circumstances, but moving with direction and clarity. It calls for consistent reflection, taking the time to learn from each season so that your experiences are not wasted but transformed into wisdom. And it demands alignment—choosing actions that reflect God's vision for your life, allowing Him to guide the unfolding of your story with intention and truth. When you begin to see life through this lens, it no longer feels random or disconnected. You start to recognize that God is intentionally placing people, opportunities, and lessons throughout your timeline, each one carrying meaning and potential for growth. But awareness alone is not enough—it is your responsibility to interpret these moments, to respond with intention, and to actively participate in shaping what your story becomes.

The Role of Reflection

Reflection is where wisdom is born, because it is in the act of looking back with intention that meaning begins to emerge from what once felt scattered. Without reflection, life can feel like a series of disconnected events—moments that happen without clear purpose, lessons that go unnoticed, and experiences that seem unrelated to one another. But with reflection, something shifts. Your life begins to take on shape, becoming a tapestry of meaning where every thread—whether joyful or painful—finds its place. When you pause to examine your victories, your failures, your transitions, your relationships, your disappointments, and your breakthroughs, you begin to see patterns, lessons, and growth that were not visible in the moment. What once felt random begins to reveal intention. What once felt confusing begins to make sense. Reflection transforms your life from fragmented to purposeful, allowing you to carry forward not just experiences, but wisdom. And in that process, you begin to notice something deeper—God's fingerprints in places you once overlooked, quietly present in every season, guiding, shaping, and revealing His hand all along.

Real-World Analogy — The Memoir in Progress

Imagine your life as a memoir being written one page at a time, each day adding a new line, a new moment, a new piece to the unfolding story of who you are becoming. You may not have control over every storm that appears or every unexpected plot twist that disrupts your plans, but you do have the power to determine the meaning you draw from those experiences. That meaning shapes the direction of your narrative. Those who choose to live intentionally begin to see hardship differently—they recognize it as character development, as necessary tension that strengthens, refines, and prepares them for what is ahead. In contrast, those who drift through life without reflection often interpret the same hardships as defeat, allowing circumstances to define their identity rather than develop it. The difference is not found in the situation itself, but in the posture of the person living through it. It is not circumstance that determines the outcome—it is authorship, the intentional decision to assign purpose, extract meaning, and continue writing your story with clarity and conviction.

Writing with Awareness

Your story is not ultimately defined by what happens to you, but by how you interpret it, how you respond to it, and how you allow it to shape your growth over time. Circumstances may be outside of your control, but your posture within them carries weight and meaning. In His sovereignty, God remains the ultimate Author of your life—nothing escapes His awareness, and nothing is outside of His design. Yet, in His grace, He chooses to consider you, to involve you, and to entrust you with real decisions that influence how your story unfolds. He places responsibility in your hands—not to override His authority, but to align with His will. You are called to live with intention, to respond with clarity, and to move with the conviction that your life carries divine significance far beyond what you can see in the moment. And now that you have embraced your role in stewarding the life God has given you, the next question becomes essential: how will your story extend beyond you, and what impact will it leave on the world around you?

Section 2: Leaving a Positive Impact on the World

Legacy Is Contribution, Not Accumulation

Legacy is not defined by what you collect, accumulate, or achieve—it is ultimately revealed by what you contribute and leave behind in the lives of others. The things the world often celebrates—titles, recognition, and status—will eventually fade. Achievements that once felt monumental will blur with time, and possessions that once held value will decay or lose significance. But influence endures. The lives you touch, the wisdom you share, and the faith you embody create a ripple effect that extends far beyond your own lifetime. These are the things that carry weight long after you are gone. Your legacy, then, is not measured by applause or public acknowledgment, but by impact—the lasting imprint of how you lived, how you loved, and how you chose to show up in the world.

The Ripple Effect of Influence

Most impact is quiet, often going unnoticed in the moment. It is invisible, slow, and subtle, not always accompanied by recognition or immediate results. It shows up in the smallest expressions—a single word of encouragement spoken at the right time, a moment of service when it was least expected, a quiet act of integrity when no one else was watching, or a simple seed planted in someone else's life through your presence, your words, or your example. These moments may seem insignificant on the surface, but they carry weight far beyond what you can see. They create ripples that extend into places you may never witness, shaping lives, influencing decisions, and inspiring growth in ways that unfold over time. You never truly know who is watching your life, who is learning from your example, or who is becoming a better version of themselves because you chose to show up with purpose, consistency, and intention.

The Four Dimensions of Impact

Your influence flows through multiple areas of life.

1. **Romantic & Personal Relationships**: Lead with love, humility, and vulnerability. Your character is most visible to those closest to you.
2. **Platonic & Community Connections**: Your presence can be someone's peace, accountability, or encouragement. Your consistency can anchor others.

3. **Professional Environment**: Lead ethically. Serve diligently. Collaborate generously. Your workplace can become a mission field without ever quoting a scripture out loud.
4. **Spiritual Influence**: Your faith is one of the greatest legacies you leave. Your obedience, transformation, and testimony can guide others toward God without preaching a sermon.

Real-World Analogy — The Garden You Tend

Imagine tending a garden, carefully planting seeds with hope, patience, and intention, knowing that not everything will grow at the same pace or in the same way. Some seeds bloom quickly, revealing their beauty almost immediately, while others remain hidden beneath the surface for years, developing quietly before they ever emerge. Some withstand storms with strength, while others require gentle, consistent care to reach their full potential. Yet every seed, regardless of its timing or visibility, contributes to the overall beauty of the garden. Your life is that garden. Every act of kindness you extend, every moment of leadership you embrace, every lesson you teach, and every example you set becomes a seed planted into the lives of others. You may not always see the results, and you may not always know the impact, but God is faithful to bring growth in His timing. What you plant today has the potential to bloom long after you are gone, creating beauty, transformation, and purpose that extends far beyond your own lifetime.

Significance Over Prominence

Legacy is not built through occasional grand gestures or singular moments of recognition—it is formed through daily decisions, the consistent choices you make when no one is watching and no applause is given. It is found in the quiet roots of influence, love, faith, and service that grow steadily over time, often unseen but deeply impactful. These roots anchor your life in something greater than yourself, allowing your actions to outlast the storms of life and echo across generations in ways you may never fully witness. What you do consistently becomes what you leave behind. And now that you understand your capacity to influence the world beyond your immediate reach, the final step is to step back and see the bigger picture—to recognize the story your life is telling, not just in moments, but across the entirety of your journey.

Section 3: Reflecting on a Life Well-Lived

Reflection Is Sacred Accountability

A life without reflection is a life that unknowingly repeats the same mistakes, overlooks the blessings that were present, and misunderstands the deeper purpose woven into each season. Without taking the time to pause and look back with intention, experiences can pass by without producing the wisdom they were meant to give. Reflection, however, is not nostalgia—it is wisdom in motion. It is not about dwelling on the past, but about drawing meaning from it. It becomes a sacred pause, a moment where you step out of the noise of life long enough for God to reveal what you may have missed, to illuminate the lessons hidden within your experiences, and to show you how you have grown. In that space, you begin to see more clearly—not just what happened, but who you have become because of it.

The Sacred Pause

God often calls you into stillness, not as a way to stop your progress, but as a way to center you—bringing your heart, your mind, and your spirit back into alignment with His purpose. In a world that constantly pushes you to move faster, do more, and stay busy, stillness becomes sacred. It is in these quiet moments that God gently redirects your focus, helping you see the significance in seasons you may have once dismissed as ordinary or unimportant. What felt routine begins to reveal meaning. What felt insignificant begins to carry weight. And in that pause, something powerful happens—your victories begin to transform into testimonies that remind you of God's faithfulness, your failures become lessons that sharpen your wisdom, your losses bring clarity that refines your direction, and your relationships reveal themselves as treasures that shaped your journey. Reflection, then, is not passive—it is transformative. It turns your experiences into revelation, allowing you to see your life through the lens of purpose rather than circumstance.

Seeing the Full Story

Your life is more than a collection of isolated moments—it is a tapestry, carefully woven together with intention, detail, and purpose. Every triumph, every trial, every transition, and every transformation adds a thread to the overall design, contributing to a picture that is far more meaningful than any single experience on its own. Some threads are vibrant and easy to celebrate, while others are darker, harder to understand, and difficult to carry. Yet each one matters. Reflection is what allows you to step back and truly see what has been created. It reveals patterns of God's provision that sustained you in ways you did not fully recognize at the time. It exposes cycles that need to be broken so that growth can take place. It highlights seeds that were planted long ago and have finally begun to bear fruit. And it brings awareness to lessons that have repeated themselves, not to frustrate you, but to develop you. When you pause long enough to take in the full picture, you begin to realize that nothing was random—God was writing beauty all along, even in the places that once felt uncertain or incomplete.

Real-World Analogy — The Artist's Retrospective

Imagine an artist standing before a massive canvas, carefully applying each brushstroke with intention. Up close, the painting may look chaotic—colors layered without clear order, strokes that seem disconnected, and patterns that do not immediately make sense. It can feel incomplete, even confusing, when viewed from that limited perspective. But when the artist steps back, something shifts. Order begins to emerge. The colors that once clashed start to reveal meaning. What looked like chaos transforms into a beautiful composition, each element working together to form a greater picture. Your life is the same. When you are standing in the middle of your experiences, it can be difficult to understand how everything connects or why certain moments unfold the way they do. But while your view is limited, God's perspective is complete. You may not be able to see the full beauty while you are still within the painting, but He can—because He is the One who sees the entire canvas at once, bringing purpose and design to every detail of your story.

Wisdom Through Reflection

Reflection is the key that unlocks gratitude, clarity, and purpose, because it allows you to see your life with understanding rather than confusion. It shifts your perspective from simply experiencing moments to truly learning from them, revealing the value in both the highs and the lows. Through reflection, gratitude begins to grow as you recognize how God has sustained you, even in seasons that once felt uncertain or difficult. Clarity begins to emerge as patterns, lessons, and direction become more visible. And purpose becomes more defined as you understand how each experience has been shaping you for what lies ahead. Reflection honors every season you have endured, acknowledging both the strength it required and the growth it produced. At the same time, it prepares your heart for what is to come, positioning you to move forward with wisdom, awareness, and a deeper sense of alignment.

Seasons Complete, Life Illuminated

You have traveled through every season of life's journey, each one leaving its mark and shaping who you have become. Spring renewed your hope, awakening dreams and possibilities you may have once thought were lost. Summer stretched you through growth and opportunity, calling you to steward what was placed in your hands with intention and courage. Autumn taught you the power of release, making room for deeper revelation and clarity as you let go of what no longer aligned. And winter forged your resilience, strengthening your faith and endurance in the moments that felt the most challenging. Along the way, you have explored identity, purpose, calling, relationships, wellness, and now—legacy. Through it all, one truth has remained constant: God has been writing your story with intention, weaving together every detail with purpose. Every triumph became a chapter that revealed His faithfulness, every setback became a subplot that refined your character, and every season played a role in shaping your becoming. You are not the same person who began this journey. You are wiser, stronger, more aware, and more aligned with your purpose than ever before. And now, as you stand in this moment of clarity, you hold the pen with a new sense of confidence, ready to move forward with intention and faith.

The Call Forward

The seasons will continue to change—that is the nature of life. There will be new beginnings that stretch your faith, unexpected transitions that test your resolve, and moments that call you to grow in ways you did not anticipate. But now, you are not walking into those seasons unprepared. You carry a roadmap. You have learned how to navigate change with clarity instead of confusion, with faith instead of fear, and with intention instead of reaction. You are no longer drifting—you are moving with purpose. And as you step into the chapters ahead, let your life reflect what you have come to understand. Write with purpose, making decisions that align with who you are becoming. Live with intention, refusing to settle for a life that is merely convenient. Love with depth, showing up fully and authentically in every relationship you are entrusted with. Serve with grace, recognizing that your impact is found in how you give, not just what you gain. Lead with humility, knowing that true strength is rooted in character, not control. Reflect with wisdom, allowing every season to shape you rather than harden you. And as you walk forward, build a legacy that reflects not only who you are in this moment, but who God has been forming you to become all along. Your story is not finished. In fact, some of the most meaningful, impactful, and transformative pages have yet to be written. They are waiting on your obedience. They are waiting on your courage. They are waiting on your yes.

ABOUT THE AUTHOR

Xavian D. Lewis is a leader, communicator, and creative committed to helping people navigate life's transitions with clarity, faith, and purpose. Through honest reflection and spiritually grounded insight, he challenges readers to see seasons of change not as setbacks, but as invitations for growth, healing, and transformation.

With a background spanning leadership, entrepreneurship, and ministry, Xavian brings a practical yet deeply reflective perspective to personal development. His work centers on emotional awareness, spiritual maturity, and the courage required to become who God is shaping you to be — especially in seasons where life feels uncertain or in motion.

Thriving In Transition reflects his passion for walking with others through the in-between spaces of life, reminding readers that growth does not require having all the answers — only the willingness to keep moving forward with intention and trust.

www.ingramcontent.com/pod-product-compliance
Lightning Source LLC
LaVergne TN
LVHW010938110826
845149LV00013B/2664
* 9 7 9 8 9 9 4 5 6 6 4 0 4 *